FOUL DEEDS AND SUSPICIOUS
DEATHS IN AND AROUND DONCASTER

TRUE CRIME FROM WHARNCLIFFE
Foul Deeds and Suspicious Deaths Series

Barking, Dagenham & Chadwell Heath
Barnsley
Bath
Bedford
Birmingham
Black Country
Blackburn and Hyndburn
Bolton
Bradford
Brighton
Bristol
Cambridge
Carlisle
Chesterfield
Colchester
Coventry
Croydon
Derby
Dublin
Durham
Ealing
Folkestone and Dover
Grimsby
Guernsey
Guildford
Halifax
Hampstead, Holborn and St Pancras
Huddersfield
Hull

Leeds
Leicester
Lewisham and Deptford
Liverpool
London's East End
London's West End
Manchester
Mansfield
More Foul Deeds Birmingham
More Foul Deeds Chesterfield
More Foul Deeds Wakefield
Newcastle
Newport
Norfolk
Northampton
Nottingham
Oxfordshire
Pontefract and Castleford
Portsmouth
Rotherham
Sheffield
Scunthorpe
Southend-on-Sea
Staffordshire and The Potteries
Stratford and South Warwickshire
Tees
Warwickshire
Wigan
York

OTHER TRUE CRIME BOOKS FROM WHARNCLIFFE

A–Z of Yorkshire Murder
Black Barnsley
Brighton Crime and Vice 1800–2000
Durham Executions
Essex Murders
Executions & Hangings in Newcastle
   and Morpeth
Norfolk Mayhem and Murder

Norwich Murders
Strangeways Hanged
The A–Z of London Murders
Unsolved Murders in Victorian and
   Edwardian London
Unsolved Norfolk Murders
Unsolved Yorkshire Murders
Yorkshire's Murderous Women

Please contact us via any of the methods below for more information or a catalogue.
WHARNCLIFFE BOOKS
47 Church Street – Barnsley – South Yorkshire – S70 2AS
Tel: 01226 734555 – 734222 Fax: 01226 734438
E-mail: enquiries@pen-and-sword.co.uk
Website: www.wharncliffebooks.co.uk

Foul Deeds & Suspicious Deaths In and Around
DONCASTER

STEPHEN WADE

True Crime

First published in Great Britain in 2010 by
Wharncliffe Local History
an imprint of
Pen & Sword Books Ltd
47 Church Street
Barnsley
South Yorkshire
S70 2AS

ISBN 978 1 84563 110 9

A CIP catalogue record for this book is available from the British
Library.

Typeset in 11/13pt Plantin by
Mac Style, Beverley, East Yorkshire

Printed and bound in the UK
by CPI Antony Rowe, Chippenham, Wiltshire

Pen & Sword Books Ltd incorporates the imprints of Pen & Sword
Aviation, Pen & Sword Maritime, Pen & Sword Military,
Wharncliffe Local History, Pen and Sword Select, Pen and Sword
Military Classics and
Leo Cooper.

For a complete list of Pen & Sword titles please contact
PEN & SWORD BOOKS LIMITED
47 Church Street, Barnsley, South Yorkshire, S70 2AS, England
E-mail: enquiries@pen-and-sword.co.uk
Website: www.pen-and-sword.co.uk

Contents

Acknowledgements

In researching a book of this kind, a great deal of help is required. Dr Charles Kelham of Doncaster Archives has been most helpful in providing illustrations. A case book like this needs a variety of images in order to reflect the range of sources. Library staff at the University of Hull have been an excellent support, also, and thanks are due to previous writers on the history of Doncaster, notably Brian Barber, author of a new standard history of the town. Staff at Doncaster Library Local Studies have been very helpful in the hunt for material in the lesser-known by-ways of crime.

A particularly unusual source (and therefore a wonderful help) for this volume has been a work by Ernest Pettifer, once Clerk of the West Riding Justices; his memoirs really opened up some dramatic and fascinating stories.

Introduction

In 1536, in the aftermath of what is now known as the Pilgrimage of Grace, a revolt against Henry VIII, a proclamation was made regarding the apparent pardons of some of the major figures involved. One of these, addressed to Cartmel Priory, read:

Neighbours of Carpmel [sic], *so it is that the King's herald hath made Proclamation here that every man, under pain of high treason, shall suffer Everything, such as farms, tithes and other such to be in like stay and Order concerning possession, as they were in the last meeting at Doncaster.*

One of the leaders of the rebellion, Yorkshireman Robert Aske, had been at a meeting in Doncaster at which pardons were arranged. The Royal Pardon was proclaimed to the heralds and so these messages went all over the country. They were worthless. Henry, having had his own *annus horribilis* in 1536, was his usual duplicitous self. The proclamation was forgotten and men were executed in large numbers across the land, including Aske himself.

This footnote to history raises the question of what 'crime' is at specific times, and also the question of 'foul deeds' being committed by those with power and authority, as well as by those who are merely ordinary citizens. The other point is that it was at Doncaster that Aske had been negotiating. That is merely one of several key moments in British history that has a link to Doncaster. As the following pages will show, other important deeds have been done here, and many of them by villains of a very high order. The murder of Rainborough in 1648 for instance, may be seen as a formative incident during the Civil War.

There have also been criminal issues in the area related to very large national questions, such the militancy of the Suffragettes and the repressive measures taken at the time of strikes. Selections had to be made: I have left out coverage of the Bag Muck Strike linked to mining communities, but I have included a story from that context involving a notably foul deed. Where I have stretched the remit a little is in retelling the amazing 'Baccarat Scandal' of 1890. Although this took place at Anlaby, near Hull, it was inextricably linked to the Doncaster St Leger meeting at the time because the Prince of Wales and his followers were there for that jaunt, and their indulgence in a game of baccarat not only hit the headlines, but became a classic crime narrative, with its own volume in the standard series of *Notable British Trials,* published by William Hodge in the 1920s and 1930s.

The cases collected here, however, concentrate mainly on everyday crime: murder, assault, fraud, rape and manslaughter being the foremost in the lists. In addition to these, there are other more borderline and contentious offences such as theft and vagrancy. But as the reader will discover with a cursory look at the chapter on the quarter sessions (Chapter 2), in years gone by the officers of the law had to concern themselves with such matters as idle constables, slander, public nuisance and disorder. These records tell a story of crime that is all too familiar, and that never seems to go away: offences through desperation, poverty, social exclusion and insanity. It is also something that makes the modern reader feel more sympathy for the justices through the centuries: so much onerous business fell at their door and they had to cope.

Doncaster, famous for railways, mining and horse racing, was often described in the early Victorian years as markedly different to other Yorkshire towns. One directory notes that 'The air is remarkably pure and salubrious, and as might be expected, the population is progressively on the increase.' By 1830, when crime rates in England were soaring and there was massive and widespread unrest in agricultural communities, as well as the agitation for suffrage reform, the population was around 10,000. In 1821, it was doing so well that one writer stated: 'There are few towns in the kingdom in which so great a portion of the inhabitants possess independent fortunes, and the neighbourhood is remarkable for opulent families.'

The races, and in particular the St Leger, have always been a main attraction and a defining feature of Doncaster's identity. Three of the stories here concern horse racing in one way or another. The historian of the turf, Patrick Chalmers, in his book, *Racing England* (1939), gave the most informative account of that identity when he wrote:

> *Doncaster, another northern meeting, is as beloved an outing for the Tykes as is Chester ... The races have held a prominent part in Yorkshire history and still they express the determination of a sport-loving community to provide the best possible racing on the best possible terms ... Doncaster draws all the north to her. The place is the centre of a horse-loving district ...*

That is true, and of course racing involves gambling, and that pastime opens up criminal opportunities. The tale of a certain John Senior in 1810 illustrates this, and his story is not uncommon in the annals of Doncaster crime. He was a clothier but, as one contemporary account of him says, '... in 1809 he associated with a variety of sporting characters and could not resist the temptation of annual visits to Doncaster and York race courses'. He was 'a great loser' and this led him to commit frauds. Senior illegally obtained £2,000 – a vast sum in 1810. He pleaded not guilty but was tried at York and sentenced to death. At the time of his trial he was bankrupt and in debt for a very large sum.

Of course, a book with the words 'foul deeds' in the title has to include murder cases, and this is no exception. In the nineteenth century, as Chapter 7 shows, there were frequent attacks on the person and homicides. Some were only sparsely reported, and so we know little of the full story, as in the tale of Frederick Cooke, only eighteen years old, who murdered his little brother, just a toddler, by striking him with a hatchet. Or the attempted murder of his wife by Robert Collinson, a collier, of Bolton-on-Dearne, in 1852: he beat his wife with a metal bar, entering the home at half past six one morning, just after being released from prison. He was found guilty of attempted murder but said in court, 'I shall have to go to prison but when I come out I shall finish her.'

Of course, the Doncaster area has a criminal history in the centuries before my main stories that tells other tales, but we know only fragments of most of these. One clue to the sheer vastness of the subject is to note a few local gaols and gallows. In Thorne, for instance, the castle was used in the sixteenth century for offenders who had poached royal game. As Malcolm Hobson has written: 'The area must have contained quite vast numbers of deer for as late as 1609 several hundred were rounded up near Tudworth for the pleasure of Prince Henry, eldest son of James I.'

As to the gallows: there were gallows before the seventeenth century at Doncaster, and in Conisbrough; and another at Tickhill, controlled by the warden of the royal castle. Not far away at Barnsley was another gallows. In the Medieval period and in the Early Modern era there were gallows in all kinds of places, some run by religious powers and others secular. When we recall that serious offences, from the thirteenth century through to the Elizabethan period, when there were major reforms after the break from Rome, were tried at the assizes or at manorial or church courts, it becomes clear why there were so many hanging places. Power and punishment could be extreme and swift – and not always done within the main system of the criminal justice of the state itself.

Of course, the medieval period in the area's history also brings to mind the most famous outlaw of them all: Robin Hood. In the 1930s, a travel writer commented on this element of a narrative that stands somewhere between history and folklore:

It is but a small detour I have made, and I regain the main road a mile or so beyond the point at which I left it ... till at last I see by the roadside a stone cupola supported on four columns, which is really much too interesting to pass by without consideration for this ... was the well of Robin Hood, so called in every ancient record we have ...

It was commented, for instance, that during the journey of Henry VIII for his coronation, he was greeted near Doncaster by 'a right great and noble company on Barnesdale, a little beyond Robin Hood's stone'.

The well is at Skellbrook, almost seven miles north of Doncaster, and the story goes that Robin robbed the Bishop of Hereford there, and then danced with joy around a tree. It's maybe not such a 'foul deed' of course, as he was going to give to the poor!

But for the majority of the cases in the book, the social history they reflect is what would be expected of a community in which all kinds of social and familial stresses weighed heavily on wage-earners doing long hours and tough work, whether that was down the pit or in engineering. One of the most common crimes for the period covering the years 1800 to c.1930 concerns domestic homicide, as in this brief report from 1895:

> *At Doncaster, on Saturday, William Dransfield, a collier, was charged with the attempted murder of his wife and also with attempting to commit suicide. The quarrel was over a lodger…*

But towards the end of the nineteenth century and in the Edwardian years, there was an emergence of more white collar crime, and also massive social problems related to juvenile delinquency and the workings of the magistrates' courts. In those years, one of the major debates was about the physical punishment of the young, and there was just as much of a gang problem then as now. The reasons are not hard to find: the breakdown of the family though hard times, the effects of heavy drinking, and the sheer monotony and drabness of the daily life of endless toil and little rest. But these were universal subjects: not confined to Doncaster of course.

I have tried to balance the material, contrasting fairly well-known stories with obscure, forgotten ones that were sensational in their time. Some locations and themes recur. One notable example is the *Salutation Inn*, which crops up as a crime scene on two occasions here. On the whole, the stories mostly concern violence, murder and cruelty, but there are a few less immediately compelling cases such as one of slander, and another, of alleged obscenity. There are also mysteries without any closure, the most puzzling being the 'Mysterious Peace Man' of Chapter 24. In a crime case book, or in any true crime biography, the reader (and the researcher) desire some kind of satisfactory completion of the drama and events surrounding the crime. With the 'Peace Man' this never happened, as far as I am aware.

Many offences were of their time, of course, and are not seen today in the same way as in their historical context. Social crime such as poaching is the classic example. I have dealt with poaching cases in the main chapters, but there are some tales which can only be called 'curiosities' and I have given those narratives in a final 'miscellany' chapter.

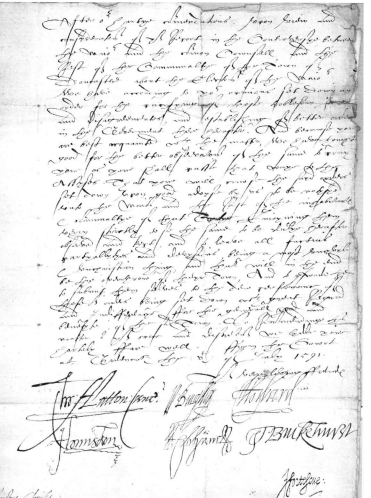

Letter from the Privy Council to Mr Justice Clinch, 1591. There was a dispute over the election of Mayor, an early legal drama. By permission of Doncaster Archives, Doncaster MBC

CHAPTER 1

A Revenge Plot in the *Bull Inn* 1582

The innkeeper played pimp to his wife, to trap Sandys.

In Elizabethan England, there was paranoia and duplicity on all sides: the Queen and government were constantly struggling to keep the balance of power in Europe, pitted against Catholic Spain. Our island status was a great advantage, but that also meant that spies and double agents were always on the move, and the coast was very hard to patrol.

The Queen needed a spycatcher, and she had a number of excellent ones, including Sir Francis Walsingham and Sir Christopher Hatton. These men recruited agents to work in their networks and to go undercover. It was not a difficult task because the universities were full of the younger sons of well-to-do men, and they needed something to do. There were always armies being raised to indulge in either suppressing the Irish or taking on Catholic armies in Europe. Spying was a good choice, too, and several amoral and two-faced rogues signed up to work in espionage.

Two of these men, Bernard Maude and Robert Poley, figure in this nasty little plot that took place in Doncaster. Maude was a graduate of Trinity College, Oxford, leaving there in 1566. Poley was a Cambridge man, but in the lowest grade, called a 'sizar' which meant he had to do some of the lowest chores around in order to have fees paid, and continue. Poley was, after these events in Doncaster, to be involved in the famous Babington Plot to murder Queen Elizabeth in 1586. Maude was to prove to be a guttersnipe born survivor, escaping from attention and retribution, even after that major political piece of skulduggery.

The tomb of Archbishop Sandys, Southwell Minster. Author's collection

In 1582, Maude was working for Sir Robert Stapleton, of Wighill. He was High Sheriff of Yorkshire at that time – a post he was to keep for just one year, such was his feckless and criminal nature. The spy had previously worked for the Cumbrian, Edwin Sandys, who had become Archbishop of York by the time of this story. He had led a colourful life, having been imprisoned in the Tower, and at one time the common people had hated him, linking him to what was then called 'Popery'. Sandys comes out of his dark years as very impressive, having said at one point, when under threat of death, 'I will yield unto God and not unto man...I have read in the scriptures of many godly and courteous keepers...God may make me one.'

But the archbishop had all kinds of enemies, and Stapleton was one. In May 1582, both Sandys and Stapleton were at the

Bull Inn. It is not clear why, but it would seem that Stapleton was looking for preferment – a cosy little job in London. Sandys had the power to arrange this but did not. He felt only contempt for the High Sheriff. Now, a man with that position in Yorkshire had a great deal of influence and authority. He was not at all happy with the rejection by this churchman, and he wanted to get even.

At the *Bull*, the spy Maude was working for Stapleton, and a plan was hatched that seems amazing in its seedy and underhand nature, even today, when we have turned cynical about the statesmen of this period; and when not being two-faced was a recipe for ruin. What happened was that Stapleton persuaded the innkeeper to arrange an embarrassing episode in which Sandys would be found in bed with the innkeeper's wife. The landlord of the *Bull* was only too pleased to help, as Stapleton crossed his palm with silver.

Thus, the *Bull's* innkeeper, William Sisson, played pimp to his wife in order to trap Sandys. Mrs Sisson slipped into Sandys' bed and then of course there was a noisy and angry confrontation as Stapleton and Maude, with their hangers-on, burst into the room and saw the archbishop's shock. His words of surprise and outrage were ignored. One report says that Sisson threatened Sandys with a dagger. The outcome was exactly what Stapleton wanted: extortion and blackmail. We have the outrageous situation then, in which the High Sheriff of Yorkshire is squeezing the Archbishop of York for huge amounts of money, to prevent a sleazy story getting out and reaching the ears of those in power at Lambeth Palace and in Parliament.

Stapleton demanded £800. In today's money that would be a million. Eventually, the archbishop paid £600. He also gave the Sheriff a lease to some property. But Sandys was not a man to lie down and take all this mildly. He still had powerful friends and he was not afraid to go and grovel. He went to the great Lord Burghley and explained what had happened. Inevitably, the Queen heard about the farce and ordered an inquiry. The money had to be paid back and another large sum had to be paid to the Queen, to keep Maude and Stapleton out of gaol. It was only a temporary respite: Maude was sent to prison for three years, but was recruited as a spy by Walsingham, who knew that the prisons were full of desperate men who would rather be in his pay than rot in a rat-infested cell.

The Stapleton crew had actually had to appear before the Star Chamber court, the place at which trials took place on 'over mighty subjects' and which became a byword for repression and tyranny. Stapleton's fate was not a happy one. As a Victorian biographer wrote:

> *They were hereupon compelled, besides other punishments, to acknowledge the Archbishop's innocence at the assizes at York. But as this submission, particularly on the part of Sir Robert, was made with little appearance of contrition, the prelate for his own justification rightly insisted on further satisfaction ... And it was not until after a long confinement in the Tower and the Fleet, that in 1584, Stapleton showed himself to be really penitent for the crime.*

It still appears that Stapleton was merely desperate to get out and try to find a place in society again. After all, here was a man who had thrown away the highest position in law and administration for the county of Yorkshire – all because he wanted to get even with a man who had rejected him and personally disliked him.

As for Edwin Sandys, he is chiefly remembered today as a writer on doctrine, and as a man always in the heat of controversy. But we have to admire the courage of a man who could say, when under threat of death, 'My life is not dear to me, neither have I done or said anything that urgeth my conscience.' This was a man who had moved from one position of high power to another, escaped the block and the axe, and lived through the changing regimes of Protestant and Catholic monarchs. But arguably the toughest challenge he ever had to his survival as a man of power was what happened that night in Doncaster.

CHAPTER 2

Lawbreakers at the Quarter Sessions c.1640

...each was burned in his left hand, according to the form of the Statute.

Sir Francis Wortley was created a baronet in 1611, and later became a Colonel of Foot fighting for the King, Charles I. But fighting and soldiering was not his only business. He, with other knights and nobles, sat on the Bench for the West Riding Quarter Sessions. These were the basic everyday workhorses of the criminal justice system in Wortley's time, and had been so since the early Middle Ages. They dealt with virtually every kind of local crime – including felonies and misdemeanours. The felonies, the serious crimes, would mean that the offenders were sent on to York Castle to be tried at York Assizes, so before Francis and his peers there could be any kind of criminal matter, from payment of constables to homicide.

Often the trouble was a brawl: these were common between the fourteenth and seventeenth centuries, as in a violent society with little effective policing, men resorted to knives and staffs if they were riled. There was such an affray at Hatfield in 1638. What happened was that Robert Lund and three other men were in legal possession of some land – common pasture – and a gang of locals didn't want them there. The inquisition was taken: the men were lawfully on the land, until 'Francis Thurley, John Chapman, Daniel Chapman and other known ill doers on the 1st May inst. With staves and swords entered the said common and by forces disseised and expelled them...' The rogues took the land and held it by force of arms. They were brought before the court, all except Daniel Chapman, who took off and would not appear. The thugs had 'disseised' the others, meaning that they had wrongfully seized freehold property.

There was also a deal of theft, breaking and entering going on: Richard Hobson, another man, and a widow called Katherine Booth, broke into a house and stole a chest of goods. The offences were mixed in this respect in October 1637: one man stole a bible worth five shillings and a butcher of Cawthorne stole six 'wethers' (sheep). Margaret Chambers stole a waistcoat, a petticoat and 'a pecke of oatemeale'. Petty theft was going on all the time, and it was often the usual opportunist business, as with two women of Brampton Brierley, who stole twelve sheaves of barley.

The 1637 sessions record a long list of crimes, mostly felonies, and so one possible punishment was death. Reading the account today, there is a deep sense of foreboding in the wording; sixteen men and two women were 'Put for good or ill upon the country, whereupon a jury was called.' We can imagine them all lined up before the twelve good men and true, waiting for their fate. The report goes on:

> *... they were led to the bar by the sheriff and asked what they could say for themselves, why they should not have judgement of death according to the law for the felonies aforesaid whereof they were convicted. They severally said that they were clerks and prayed for benefit of clergy to be granted them.*

What happened next was going on along the length and breadth of the land. The 'Benefit of Clergy' ruling meant that if a felon could read what was called the 'neck verse' – which they could claim on only one occasion, then they would be branded rather than hanged. The neck verse was the opening of the 51st Psalm: 'Have mercy upon me, O God, according to Thy loving kindness: according to the multitude of Thy tender mercies blot out my transgressions.'

The neck verse was originally intended to give clergy an exemption from the criminal law process. An old poem explains:

If a clerk had been taken
For stealing of bacon,
For burglary, murder or rape.
If he could but rehearse
(well prompt) his neck verse,
He never could fail to escape.

But the unhappy line of men and women in 1637, although they had learned the words well, had further pain to come. By a law of Henry VII they had to be branded: each was burned in his left hand, according to the Statute. It said: 'Every person so convicted of murder, be marked with an M upon the brawn of the left thumb, and if he be convicted for any other felony the same person to be marked with a T in the same place upon the thumb, and these marks to be made by a gaoler openly in court before the judge.' There were screams of agony that day in the courtroom.

At the same session, Sir Francis himself was facing a man who had committed a crime on the good lord's land. Ralph Greaves of Bolsterstone went into the deer park of Sir Francis at 'New Parke', Wortley and went with his greyhounds to hunt the judge's deer. He was lucky to escape with a large fine. But if we are looking for ironies, then there is a coda to the story of Sir Francis and New Park. According to the notorious diarist Oliver Heywood, that land had been forcefully taken from the Wortley family by Sir Francis' great-grandfather. Heywood wrote: 'Sir Francis Wortley's great-grandfather, being a man of great estate, was owner of a town near to him, only there were some freeholders on it, with whom he wrangled and sued until he beggared them and cast them out on their inheritance ...'

That has to be one of the most twisted and bitter ironies ever in a courtroom. But it is doubtful that the deer hunter, Greaves, knew anything about that nefarious local history attached to the man who was trying him from the Bench.

CHAPTER 3

The Rainsborough Murder
1648

It is probable that the murder of Rainsborough changed the course of English history ...

On 29 October 1648, Colonel Thomas Rainsborough was in Doncaster, staying in a place that should have been safe for him, yet he was killed by armed men, and history has given us different accounts of that murder. But the most likely seems to be that Rainsborough's captain of the guard was not at his post when a strong party of Royalists rode into town from Pontefract Castle. The captain was, it was said, 'at a whore-house in the town', and three other guards were apparently asleep.

The Royalists arrived at about eight in the morning, and they said that they were there to deliver a letter from Cromwell. We might ask why it would take a party of over forty men to deliver a letter, but that did not occur to whatever guards were around the place, and the Royalists went into Rainsborough's room. A door had been left open and it was an easy task to grab him, with some of the troops having their pistols drawn. The colonel was taken downstairs, saying, 'Now gentlemen, what is your business?'

It seems almost certain that a kidnap was their main intention, but Rainsborough resisted and would not go with them. He said he would rather die. Matters were soon out of hand when the prisoner refused to mount his horse and called for help from a guard who was nearby. The Royalists turned nasty and one man stabbed Rainsborough who was wounded but wanted to fight on and called for a sword. He was run through his body and one of the attackers shouted for him to be shot. One report says that Rainsborough, though severely wounded, got to his feet as the killers mounted and began to

Murder of Rainsborough. From John Tomlinson's Doncaster from the Roman Occupation to the Present Time *(1887).* By permission of Doncaster MBC

run off; he shouted at them and they turned back to finish him. It is said that he was stabbed eight times. A maid in the house heard the colonel cry out, 'I am betrayed! I am betrayed!' What seems obvious now, with hindsight, is that it was all meant to happen. Not only was the captain of the guard absent and some asleep, but no other men came to his aid, and it is certain that the struggle lasted around ten minutes.

A version told by a Royalist, published a long time after the events, makes sense in that it insists that the plan was to take

Cavaliers after the Rainborough murder. Author's collection

Rainsborough hostage and keep him at Pontefract. A prominent and popular Royalist leader, Sir Marmaduke Langdale, was a prisoner at Nottingham, and an exchange was intended. Two brothers called Paulden led this enterprise, and this account states that the gang stopped at Mexborough, rested, and then sent a spy to Doncaster to check on the state of affairs with regard to Rainsborough's situation. Then they entered the town under the pretence of being from a regiment led by one White and said they had a letter from Cromwell. The Paulden gang told the colonel that they would not harm him if he went quietly with them. The story went that Rainsborough yelled out 'Arms!', and so a fight started.

This account says that one man from Paulden's group wrestled Rainsborough to the ground, trying to hold him rather than attack or kill him, but then one of Rainsborough's own men came and accidentally stabbed him; this was then followed by a deadly sword wound when it was seen that there was never going to be a hostage. Paulden had split his force of over twenty men into smaller groups and positioned them at strategic points in Doncaster. It was a very well-conceived plan, except for the fact that Rainsborough did not have the temperament to give in and accept his becoming a hostage. The account from Paulden says:

> *A cornet which was one of our four running after him and not willing to kill him caught him by the waistcoat; and in the struggle Rainsborough got his sword and Rainsborough's lieutenant his pistol but Rainsborough was thrown down and one of our troopers run him through the throat with his sword...*

So one story says that there was an officer trying to defend the colonel, and another that says Rainsborough simply faced the gang alone and his death warrant was when he screamed out an alarm.

The wider picture at the time is interesting. First, it has to be noted that Rainsborough, a man of the 'left' in the sense that he was a man with what were then called 'Leveller' views, wanting Charles I dead and a new society created with more equality. Cromwell took more of a middle position politically, and he had a more extreme pro-King arm represented by Fairfax. In all this political disagreement, it has to be pointed out that there had been an earlier attempt to kill Rainsborough. At that time he was at St Albans, and had just ruthlessly executed two Royalist leaders called Lucas and Lisle. This extremist action made him enemies: he only had one captain with him as he rode to London, and three men assaulted him. But Rainsborough and his officer put up a good fight and the would-be killers rode off.

Colonel Rainsborough was certainly disliked by many and hated by some; a contemporary ballad written after his death at Doncaster called *Colonel Rainsborough's Ghost*, shows his unpopularity:

> *Witness the bloody fights in Kent:*
> *The siege of Colchester likewise;*
> *I served well the parliament,*
> *All deeds of mercy did despise.*
> *For when the town they did surrend*
> *I plotted all against them then;*
> *I quickly brought unto an end*
> *The lives of two brave gentlemen ...*

What was the truth of all this then? Did Cromwell or some other party in the Parliamentarian forces want Rainsborough dead? Or was it just a hostage attempt that went terribly wrong? The historian, Hugh Ross Williamson, says that some interesting information about where Rainsborough was and how he was defended had got into the possession of the assassins, if that is what they were. He was staying at a prominent inn by the market place, a tavern run by a man called Mawood. We know that he had told Mawood what his plans were for the day on which he was attacked and killed – and this included the statement, 'I expect order but am uncertain.'

Williamson suggests that the party of Royalists were actually Roundheads in disguise. When they rode off they shouted, 'Farewell Rainsborough, farewell Cavaliers!' He says that they could have shouted that as soon as their disguise did not matter any longer.

Whatever the truth of the whole affair, one thing is certain: Doncaster market place was the scene of a murder – and a significant one. 'It is probable that the murder of Rainsborough changed the course of English history,' says Williamson.

The story, as Paulden told it, is the one which has been passed down into popular narrative history. Paulden's account was retold in the travel guides and journeys through Yorkshire in the Victorian and Edwardian years and, as late as 1930, in a book called *Highways and By-Ways of Yorkshire*, the author accepts that there was no assassination attempt – merely a romantic bunch of bold Cavaliers outwitting the Roundheads but bungling the hostage attempt; and seeing Rainsborough die in an accidental way in the midst of a fight. The writer says, 'Thus this bold plot miscarried through the obstinacy of a hot-headed man who … positively would not let himself be kidnapped.'

It is hard not to see the murder, however, as a very convenient death for the trajectory of the Cromwell cause.

CHAPTER 4

Father and Son Hanged
1828

He knew a brother meant to slay a brother ...

William Dyon was born in 1783, and he had a brother, John. They were sons of a Lincolnshire farmer, and the two boys were so different that this tale almost attains a biblical resonance, with jealousy, brooding resentment, and finally a deathly hatred that led one brother to a bloody death; and the other to the scaffold. It is a Cain and Abel story, but with one more layer of evil: William Dyon was joined by his son, John, in the murder.

William and his son John harboured a hatred of William's brother John, and accounts confirm that of these two murderers, William, the father, engendered in his son an irrational hatred of his uncle. The enmity grew over the years until one day when it appeared that young John had been robbed of his inheritance, and William Dyon determined to take the life of his brother. The decision to kill the man who was brother to one and uncle to the other was something that was a conclusive thought – the last line in a long line of deep and bitter enmity. This all came from the fundamentally opposite characters of the two brothers.

From their early days, William and John Dyon were conflicting personalities. One early writer on the case explains this: 'William was of a wild disposition and addicted to low sports; in his youth a frequenter of cocking matches, bull baits and so on ... and doubtless in those scenes acquired those feelings and habits that ultimately brought him to the gallows.' It was a case of the good son and the prodigal son: as John worked hard and won his father's respect, William lived a life of dissipation. Naturally, as time passed, the rift between the two brothers widened, and things were made much worse

MURDER.

THE LIVES AND TRIAL
OF

WILLIAM AND JOHN DYON.

The brother with a desperate hand
His brother's blood had shed,
And gath'ring crowds beheld him stand
Beside that brother dead.
What pangs were in that murderer's thought,
Viewing the wreck his hands had wrought.

WILLIAM DYON, the eldest son of a Mr. Dyon, a Lincolnshire farmer, was born in the year 1783, received a common education, and his attention in early life was turned to agricultural pursuits : he had a brother, named John Dyon, with whom in infancy he lived in the bonds of fraternal friendship. William was of a wild disposition, and addicted to low sports ; in his youth, a frequenter of cocking matches, bull baits, &c. and doubtless in such scenes acquired those feelings and habits that ultimately brought him to the gallows. He who commences by torturing animals for sport, too frequently ends in slaughtering his fellow-beings for gain. Whilst William was thus involved in scenes of riot and dissipation, his brother was assisting their father in the affairs of the farm. The docility of the one was, of course, preferred to the recklessness of the other ; and the praises bestowed by the parent upon John, were looked on by William as marks of favouritism. The affection of a father is the common property of his children, and should be equally divided ; but where a son forfeits his claim by

The Dyons – account of their trial at York, from WL Rede, York Castle (1829).
Author's collection

when the father left sixty-three acres of land to John in 1819. This was followed by advances in cash as well, as the father saw that he had to help and encourage the worker and ignore the wastrel.

It is not difficult to imagine the development of resentment into thoughts of murder. William fed his son John all the worst stories about his brother; he 'educated his son in an unnatural hatred of his uncle and grandfather', as a writer in 1830 put it. The last straw was the will of William senior: this was virtually all in favour of John.

Time passed, and eventually, in early February 1828, the decision to kill was made. The killers planned the attack carefully, having an assistant called White who helped them to store some arms ready for an attack on the unsuspecting John Dyon. They had left the guns in position eight days before Dyon came home, on 16 February, and set about him after his day at Doncaster market. With regard to White, it was rightly said at the time, after the trial, just how callous this assistant in murder was. Leman Rede said this: 'The conduct of this man is one of the inexplicable things that make us shudder at the baseness of humanity.' This is because White knew what the father and son had planned, and he had known John Dyon well for many years: he knew he was a good, family man, and he knew that he was playing his part in making that good man's death leave a widow and children. Rede put it simply and strongly when he wrote of White: 'He knew a brother meant to slay a brother...'

John Dyon left Doncaster with two friends, but they left him at the top of Austerfield Lane and John Dyon rode to his home at Brancroft. One writer at the time calculated that he was only 800 yards from home when the killers struck. He was shot by his gate as he dismounted to open it. His own brother and nephew had taken his life. His wife was waiting in vain for his return, and after a while a servant was sent out: this man found John's mare tied to the gate, and took the horse home. He had not seen the body of his master lying quite near. He and another servant then went out again, and this time they found the body, stiff and cold, killed heartlessly by his own relatives.

An inquest was held, and there was some suspicion cast towards the Dyons, as the enmity between the brothers was well known in the area. But a verdict of 'wilful murder by person or persons unknown' was returned. The Dyons were interviewed and they provided an alibi. But there was a reward offered for information leading to the arrest of the killers, and

York Assizes and prison cells. The author'

the man White came forward, spoke to the magistrate Denison, and the Dyons were arrested. They produced witnesses to swear that they had an alibi – that they had been in bed when the murder happened. Although a verdict at the inquest had the words 'murder by persons unknown', it was very clear to the authorities who were the main suspects.

One reason why the arrest was so straightforward was that the men had been seen by so many people on that fateful day: several men saw them and described them, and a magistrate called Denison actually did some basic scene of crime work – something very rare in those days. Denison went to the field and traced footsteps. He found the spot where they had stood, sixteen feet from a gate. He said, 'I traced some footsteps in Tommy Norton's field down to the road; they had for a certain distance walked one on each side of the hedge. The footsteps of one were made by a right and left shoe or boot; the other appeared as if the wearer turned out his toes very much. William Dyon's walk corresponds with the marks; he turns his toes out.'

We have to feel for the father of the two brothers; his favourite had been killed, and his other son arrested for the murder. But within a few days, the Dyons were in the dock in York. The surgeon gave an account of how the man had died: a bullet had penetrated his left side by a rib and had passed through the lungs. He had taken a bullet from the left shoulder blade and, when examined, the man had been dead for perhaps six hours. White was the one with most to say, naturally. White was a labourer to the dead man, and it seems possible that he fabricated much of the story he told at York, since it reads in such an embellished way. He said that they told him they had come to murder his master, and that he had got their property; and they could bear it no longer.

Other witnesses then explained how a feeble alibi had been arranged; some overheard words being said that set up an alibi within friends and family. It was even reported that William Dyon had said to one man, 'We are going to shoot your master tonight and if you tell I'll shoot you all.' The magistrate and another man both spoke of tracing the steps of two men from the Dyon gate to a distance of sixteen feet, and that they knew that William Dyon 'walked with his toes turned out'; and that the marks suggested that footprint.

William Dyon had obviously been so burning with rage and resentment that he had let others know his feelings. Samuel Kelsey from Moreton gave evidence, saying that he had met John in Gainsborough a few weeks before the murder. He said that John had told him that the old man in Lincolnshire had left John, his uncle, about £30,000, then added, 'But you will see how it will be done...'

There was no real defence, and when William Dyon was asked what he had to say, he said he left that to his counsel. The defence statements were very thin: merely remarks about there not being any guns around the house and that William Dyon was always in bed early. The jury took eight minutes to decide on a guilty verdict. Baron Hullock, presiding, said, 'A very short period remains before you suffer the sentence of the law... You must not flatter yourselves that you will experience the slightest indulgence.' By that he was partly referring to allowing their corpses to have a proper burial rather than go to the doctors for anatomical study. He also implied that an appeal for a pardon was impossible.

In those days when hangings were popular pastimes for the mob, this was a particularly popular attraction. Leman Rede wrote: 'The dreadful and extraordinary circumstances of the murder had brought thousands to the spot of its perpetration...'; then, later at the gallows, '...the crowd was markedly large and vociferous... Such was the sensational nature of this offence.'

At the scaffold, there was considerable drama, too. 'Father and son stood together, and as a prayer was read, the son joined in, with great fervency', but William stood silent. When the Under Sheriff went close to William and said, 'Your last moment is at hand, you are about to go into eternity. Do you acknowledge the justice of your sentence?' John said, 'Yes,' but his father was still angry and hard; when the cap was placed on William's head he said, 'The Lord will pardon my sins.' It took the father three minutes to die on the end of the rope; the son took twice as long, struggling and kicking. The bodies were dissected by the anatomists and their skins tanned.

Summing up, it has to be said that the killers must have known that there were no other suspects; to have done this callous murder so clumsily, having been seen by half a dozen workers and passers-by, and to have spoken openly of their rankling hatred of the industrious brother, that has to make the murder of John Dyon one of the most idiotic and self-defeating actions in the annals of British murder. In the language of the time, this was a tale that could explain what happens when 'family discord' is allowed to grow inside the spirit, to eat away at a person's humanity. As the poet William Blake wrote in his poem, *The Poison Tree* : 'I was angry with my foe / I told it not, my wrath did grow / now in the morn outstretched I see / my foe outstretched beneath a tree.'

CHAPTER 5

The Doncaster Betting-Room Robbery
1829

I would pay £500 to have that man transported!

It would be no difficult matter to fill an entire volume with crime stories linked to Doncaster races. The history of the town has a lively record of trouble brewing there for all kinds of reasons. In 1850, there was even a meeting at the Guildhall to suppress the races entirely. A number of clergymen and prominent dissenters attended and gave speeches; but they struggled to be heard, because, as *The Times* reported, 'The assemblage was, however, chiefly composed of the working classes and it was evident from the very first that they were bent on "smashing the meeting".' Things were made more chaotic when a Chartist called Charles Buckled created mayhem. It was just one scene of near anarchy in a long history of confrontation and confusion.

Reasons are not hard to find: the races have always been places where gambling is the main intention of the event of course, and where there is hazard and risk there will be fights, injustice and factions in opposition. In the Regency years there was a special interest in horse racing: the Princes of Wales have almost all taken an interest in the turf (we shall meet the most famous in Chapter 15) and the Regency period was a time when all kinds of violent sport and competitive confrontation were popular. It was an age of bear-baiting, dog-fighting and card-playing, with men often gambling away their inheritance. Often duels would be fought over questions of honour and dishonour on the turf or 'at the tables'.

The year 1829, momentous for several reasons in the history of crime, including Peel's Police Act, was the year in which

The St Leger Grandstand. Author's collection

arguably Doncaster's biggest high-profile racecourse related crime was perpetrated. It involved an infamous owner of a London 'flash house', a trial at York Castle and a notable acquittal. The crime in question was a theft of a huge amount of cash, mostly in Bank of England and local banks' notes, taken from a chest which had been unlocked by a specially made second key.

The tale begins in a betting house. It was owned by a Mrs Wilde in Doncaster. She had changed her name in the year between the crime and the trial at York, so that tells some kind of secondary story: in 1829 she was 'Mrs King'. The betting rooms were rented during the race meetings, often by wealthy men from other cities and towns. On this occasion, her rooms were rented by John Goodred and Charles Black, two Londoners who had come north for a racing break and, of course, a business enterprise, taking bets. The betting rooms were described in a report of the York trial:

> *... there are three rooms, one on the ground floor, and two above. The large room will hold 1,000 persons. There is a recess in a room – which is used as a bar. A small partition, four feet high. Parts the bar and room ...*

Thursday 17 September was big race day: the Doncaster Cup was run. The two London men secured their cash in a large chest which was placed underneath a bar counter. Before going to watch the race, Goodred made sure the chest was locked: there was almost £2,000 inside in notes and also bags of sovereigns totalling almost £400. Then he detailed a young man called Watson, who was just eighteen, to guard the box and not under any circumstances to allow anyone near it. That was his big mistake.

When Goodred returned from the track to the rooms he found that the chest was open and the money gone. He had been away from the betting rooms for two and a half hours. It was four-thirty when he returned, and he was with a man called Isiah Smart, who owned a 'flash house in Brydges Street, Covent Garden', and who was to be suspected of the theft later. The report in the *Annual Register* for 1830 describes what happened next:

> *On discovering that the money was gone, witness was in a great state of confusion, and he believed he charged Watson with being privy to the robbery ... between two and three o'clock in the morning he sent for a watchman named Seaton, to whom he gave Jenkins in charge ... he was in a small room between the betting room and the staircase, and appeared to be drunk.*

What was happening was profound confusion. Goodred was happy to blame anyone. When he had come back from the track he was with Smart, but he began to believe that Smart had arranged it all, and had paid this man, Jenkins, and possibly also Watson, to do the deed.

On further investigation, it transpired that, as the lock had not been forced but opened by a key, someone must have had a second key cut. A report just after the first response to the robbery, in the *Morning Chronicle*, described what happened next, when Smart, because of his London reputation as what we would now call a 'playboy', was in trouble:

'We have to announce that Smart, the proprietor of the 'Flash' oyster rooms in Covent Garden, was taken into custody on a late hour on Saturday night, in virtue of a warrant against him taken out by Mr Webster, the Mayor of Doncaster...Smart, it appears, had had a disagreement with several proprietors of flash houses in the vicinity of St Pauls' and Piccadilly...' The tale given to the press was that Smart was in trouble with these other businessmen, and that they were prosecuting him; that he was taking revenge on them by tit for tat proceedings. His enemies in London fixed it for the Lord Mayor to arrest their enemy. The report goes on: 'Smart readily surrendered himself to the custody of the officer and remained in St Paul's watch-house until one o'clock yesterday.' The man Jenkins was a waiter, supposedly in the pay of Smart, so Smart and Jenkins were both on their way to York to await trial at the assizes. But Smart was a rich and influential man. His solicitor was already with him in Doncaster.

As to the entry to the chest, it was discovered that a firm called Woods of Sheffield, had been asked to make a key by a man 'who had the appearance of a butcher', and that the key must have been taken away at about two o'clock on the day of the robbery – when Smart was with Goodred and plenty of others at the racetrack. The supposed villain had a sound alibi, and the real thief was now accounted for if only in a rough description given by the Sheffield locksmith.

Smart was released, but he did stand trial at York, along with Jenkins. It was reported that Smart, on realising what was going on at the betting rooms, had a definite suspect in mind: a man called Maddon. Smart said, 'I would pay £500 to have that man transported!' Jenkins had confessed that Maddon had the money but that he, Jenkins, had been complicit and had taken a cut.

Smart, the main suspect all along, was able to further exonerate himself by verifying where the money he had on him when arrested and searched came from. Basically, he was a man who was accustomed to carry large amounts of money in rolls of notes: that is what top-notch gamblers who live by gaming do. The trial report explains what was done with regard to this money:

> ...*the next morning another search was done at Smart's lodgings, when he produced £90 in Bank of England notes, and said his son had £200 in sovereigns, which he produced in a silk bag. He was asked what money he had of his father's and he replied 200 sovereigns...He said he had brought them from London.*

What was really impressive for the jury, and may have been staged by the crafty Smart, was that the father challenged the son on this and said, 'Oh no William, you did not...I gave you them at Birmingham.'

'Oh dear, aye you did...I recall now!'

The end of the trial was complete exoneration of Isiah Smart: although he kept a 'flash house' – a place where rather high-class prostitutes could be available – the Doncaster robbery could not be nailed on him. At that time, of course, any questionable morally unsound lifestyle or business could have a man condemned in the dock even before his case was presented. But Smart was acquitted: the report from York ran: '...he was, as to pecuniary matters, an honest man, and that he accompanied Bishop, the Bow Street officer, to Birmingham, and other places, and did all in his power to apprehend Maddon. The jury found the prisoners not guilty.'

Maddon remains the mystery man in this long and complex case of a daring and clever robbery, committed at a time when no questions were asked by locksmiths when a customer came to have a key cut for a chest: why should they? Some high-profile cases in the City of London in the 1870s were to revolutionise lock-making and to make the cutting of keys much more difficult to do. But in 1829, the society around gambling and gaming was one of risk, amateur protection and very foolish trust in all kinds of dodgy characters who hung around on the fringe of the racing circles. After all, Mrs King's betting rooms held a thousand men. It was not a difficult task for the robber to arrive with the copied key and have a friend distract the guard. The boy Watson was probably distracted by a bribe, or, maybe, and less nefariously, simply with an innocent-seeming game or conversation by a clever accomplice in the theft.

CHAPTER 6

Regency Mysteries and Rogues

A stake had been passed between his neck and neckerchief.

The 1820s and 1830s in England were dangerous times. In the aftermath of the war with Napoleon, times were hard, and there were all kinds of new versions of political repression, such as the laws of sedition; and epidemics of rural crime. In 1826, *The Gentleman's Magazine* had announced that there were 'riots and distresses in the country' and commented that in the manufacturing districts of Yorkshire and Lancashire there was 'the greatest distress'. The dragoon guards had been called out to deal with a mob in Accrington. But in Doncaster it was a time when the notable crimes were in almost every category, including one 'murder' that never was.

These happened in the context of a period in which a great deal of crime was attached to the range of barbarous sports the people indulged in. For instance, in 1826, there was a 'Great Rat Match' at the Westminster Pit at which a greyhound snapped up a gang of rats 'with great rapidity'. A 'chicken match' was to be fought, an announcement said, 'at the cock-pit, Millbank'. It was altogether a bloody, violent time to be alive in these islands.

But it was also a time of regular frauds. The provincial banks were at this time quite easily duped by fraudsters who could obtain signatures of well-known local dignitaries and then forge cheques. Typical of this was the tale of a travelling rogue called John Durden – a man who fades away into the fog of anonymity after being given bail. Durden had been in trouble in London before he came north; he had appeared at Bow Street Magistrates' Court in 1835, and that was after some criminal activity in Doncaster for which a warrant had been issued. A successful policeman called Leadbitter grabbed him and took him into custody, but he was not imprisoned.

Durden came to Doncaster again and went on with his fraudulent tricks. He had presented two cheques at a Doncaster company called Leatham, a bank. When he first turned up, he explained that the cheque, for over £500, was from a man called James Bromley of Goole. The cashier knew that name and he also knew the signature, so he gave Durden the cash. The rogue spun a yarn about his selling some property to Bromley, and he said the same again when he returned later, this time with the massive sum of £2,500. The cashier gave him an advance on this, of £1,000. But suspicions were emerging then; it was learned that Mr Bromley's account was overdrawn, and then enquiries around the Goole area proved that there was in fact no property of Bromley's around there.

Durden was finally arrested. He was an ironmonger from Reading, and travelled the land creating false documents and cheques, after finding ways of obtaining signatures of important figures in the regions. But at Doncaster Magistrates' Court, after Durden had been in gaol for three weeks, his lawyer demanded that a charge be made and that he be committed to York if there was definite evidence; otherwise he would have to demand bail. In the end, Mr Justice Parke sorted it out with a writ, giving Durden bail. There is no record of him after that in any source. He must have absconded, and if he was later arrested and imprisoned, he was using a false name.

In Doncaster at this time, many of the crimes and legal issues were related to finance: fraud, gambling, gaming and bankruptcy or debt. In 1828, there was even a row among the magistrates and local dignitaries. It was all about the tolerance of gaming tables during the race weeks. Because the magistrates had not suppressed the gaming tables, some do-gooders confronted them. Alderman Sheardown presented the case for abolition by saying that if there was a riot over gambling, when there were around 20,000 visitors to the town – mostly in drink – what could Doncaster do? He asked, 'Would our hundred constables do? No, it would require a regiment of soldiers.'

The magistrates didn't like this challenge to their authority. The members of a new association formed to stop gambling lost the day. A report at the time commented: 'The members of the Association, finding that the current was against them, retired, and were very roughly handled in their retreat. The tables, therefore, are to be continued under proper restriction.'

Of course, the 1820s brought plenty of serious crime as well. One of the worst was an attack on a man called Joseph Stevenson, of Harworth, near Tickhill. The poor man was a poultry keeper for Lord Viscount Galway, at Bawtry. In the early hours of one morning he set off home and was viciously attacked and robbed. He was found later that morning, with hands and feet trussed, and a stake had been passed between his neck and a neckerchief. The brutal assailant had tried and failed to strangle his victim, in a very rough makeshift way.

But the Regency years also provide us with the strangest 'crime' in Doncaster annals. The headline on the morning of 12 January 1829, in the *Morning Chronicle* reads, 'Curious Investigation as to a Supposed Murder.' A Mr Wood had disappeared some years before a skeleton was found on the racecourse, and the bones were sent to the amateur forensic scientist of the day, a Dr Buckland, for his opinion. That doctor then brought in the famous Dr Clift of the Royal College of Surgeons, and they decided that the bones had been interred for a period of between seven and ten years.

Dr Clift wrote an assessment that was unusually thorough for those times, and Buckland wrote a summary of this for the Doncaster aldermen. The doctors thought it was the skeleton of a female between the ages of sixteen and twenty-one, so that ruled out the possibility of it being Mr Wood – or so it seemed at first. But then it was noted that the person would have carried his or her head to one side and that there was a notable protrusion of the teeth in one specific spot. A man who had known George Wood said that the note about the teeth fitted Wood's characteristic, but he had his doubts about the carriage of the head. Reading the discussion today, with out knowledge of forensic anthropology, some of this is laughable. But everyone concerned agreed at the end of the debate that it could not be said with any certainty that this was the body of someone who had died violently and by unnatural causes. Was it a murder? It was an open question.

Surely the most bizarre Regency offence happened at the West Riding Sessions in Doncaster, in February 1829. What was most odd was that the villain in question was not in the dock, nor was he a witness. He was, in fact, a lawyer. He was Mr John Stringer, a Doncaster attorney, and he deliberately poured a large amount of laudanum into a glass of brandy and water at the Sessions, and then drank it all.

It was a public suicide attempt, and it succeeded. The report in the papers at the time said that 'he drank it off in the presence of the company, who were not aware of the nature of the fatal mixture until it was swallowed'. There was a rush for a doctor and in desperation someone tried to use a stomach pump to save the man, but he died around seven hours later, at five in the morning. He had in fact, committed a felony, and so his possessions and land would have been forfeit, strictly by the law, but there is no record of that being enforced.

In the last years of the Regency, Doncaster had an assortment of the strangest and most unusual criminal or possibly criminal events. Alongside the footpads and robberies, the frauds and the confrontations, there was a whole bizarre spectrum of odd and disturbing events: the next few years were to bring serious riots, arson, and cattle maiming in the countryside to the east of the town, but it is comforting to know that the most sensational events in the late Regency were not necessarily all as evil and horrendous as the Dyon murder.

In fact, one crime was perhaps the saddest of this horrendous time: a suicide at the *Salutation Inn* in South Parade. James Lucas hanged himself in that establishment in the last week of May 1828. He wrote a melancholy suicide note which read: 'James Lucas, Willow Field, near Halifax. What I owe I hope I shall be forgiven. The mare and foal are at the *Salutation*, Doncaster. I had when I left home £5.7s 6d – the bridle I will leave here – I have the dog – it may stay here too – I hope it will be taken care of for Charles Simpson –and he will take care of it for my sake – God bless you all. '

He then added a list of all his debts. His last words heard spoken before leaving home were, 'When I get to Doncaster I don't care…'

CHAPTER 7

A Gallery of Victorian Crime

Damn her ... is she dead?

The long reign of Queen Victoria (1837–1901), saw a notable change in patterns of crime. In the later decades of the period, there was a marked increase in white collar crime, but that is not to say that it was not a violent society. Before the middle years of the Queen's reign there had been all kinds of crime waves often related to radical discontent and the massive movements for reform, such as Chartism. Then, in 1861, the Offences Against the Person Act sorted out the various definitions of assault and homicide.

At the time of that Act, there was an awareness that a different type of assault was coming through – garrotting. Gangs of three or four villains would work in a team to attack and rob their victims, with one man choking the hapless individual as others robbed his person. This was reported widely throughout 1862 in particular. The main culprits were supposedly the 'Ticket of Leave Men' who had returned from transportation after that ceased in 1857. This was a concept similar to our 'release on licence' today.

In Doncaster the year 1860 was remembered in Upton for the callous murder of Elizabeth Mitchell, who worked as a farm servant for a Mr Spink of Upton farm. When Mr and Mrs Upton returned home on Sunday 2 September, they found Elizabeth lying dead on the floor. She had been shot. There was an inquest, and a local constable had a clear suspect called Thorpe, whom he detained for questioning. There was a witness against Thorpe, who said that Thorpe and the girl had argued and there had been a scuffle; Elizabeth had grabbed Thorpe by the hair and restrained him, as he was bent on attacking Mrs Cookson, who worked at the farm and who was interfering in the fight.

Thorpe said, 'Damn thee, thou'll be quiet!' and he left the house, being away for an hour. When he came back he threatened Cookson and her sister, who had had enough and left the place. But Cookson returned at about six that evening and found the body. When Thorpe was told later about Elizabeth, he said, 'Damn her, is she dead? I left her about an hour ago.' The young man was charged and on his way to York Assizes, but he escaped the noose and was imprisoned for life.

There were people falling out and resorting to fisticuffs and worse in all kinds of places. In 1873, at the cattle market, a dealer called George Crawshaw assaulted Isaac Ward, a farmer from Stainton; Ward had brought fifty sheep to sell, but there was an argument about the desired price for them. Crawshaw started a real problem when he said simply, 'We have bought these sheep,' and started driving them out of the pen. Ward grabbed him by the collar and things got out of hand: Crawshaw struck Ward hard on the head.

In court it was said that a man called Downing had bought the sheep, with the intention of immediately selling them on to Crawshaw at a profit, of course. The defence was obviously that Crawshaw was incensed by this and reacted. The argument was that Crawshaw had just 'shoved away' Ward, but that was not accepted and the magistrate ordered him to pay a ten shilling fine and fifty shillings in costs. His bad temper had cost him dearly.

Crawshaw was not the only one at this time to go out of control and end up in the dock. James Hart was also in court for assault and attempted robbery in 1868. Hart actually escaped with no punishment as there was a mix-up in the legal process. His defence argued that there was only one witness and the case was 'only a light one'. The jury had been discharged and it was too late to assemble another. There was a not guilty decision – but Hart was still deep in trouble, in Wakefield, where a bill had been issued by the Grand Jury. His fate was prison, but the Doncaster fiasco had merely delayed that inevitable fate.

In September 1875, there was a vicious act of revenge on a magistrate. Magistrate James Montague had been working at Rotherham Petty Sessions and decided to take a walk home through Melton Park. He heard the sound of branches and looked up. There he saw Aaron Cooper at the top of an elderberry tree, throwing fruit down to a woman below, who was holding a basket. Montague told him to get down and said to the woman that she would have to go with him and explain what she was doing, as he was a magistrate.

Cooper was in no mood to accept this. He was in a rage, and he took the magistrate by the throat and started to choke him; he then threw him down and sat on him, pulling an arm around the back of his victim. Eventually, Montague wrestled himself free. At the height of the struggle Cooper had shouted, 'You're in for it, and we will have it out!'

The attacker was rewarded with two months' hard labour behind bars for this savage attack.

He was joined in gaol by two colliers who attacked a Mr George Booth at Conisbrough. The men, called Wharmsley and Wattam, committed a violent assault on Booth. At the first hearing Booth was too ill to attend court. But when they were finally able to face their accuser, their destiny was assured and they were in gaol for six months.

One noticeable crime that recurs in the last few decades of the nineteenth century is cruel assaults on children at school or in other forms of social care. The Education Acts throughout the century had gradually formed a tough regimen of learning by fear as well as by rote in the monitorial system. There were frequent cases in which the pedagogues went too far with the use of the rule and the cane.

In 1896, a school mistress was in front of the bench charged with assault. Kathleen Burgess taught at Christ Church Branch School in Wellington Street. There were many rules in school of course, and one of these was that children who made a noise with their shoes had to take them off. Little George Emmerson, seven years old, made a noise but refused to take off his shoes. He was punished with the cane, and a Mrs Margetts in a house nearby heard his loud screams. A postman passing by looked into the schoolroom window and he said to Mrs Margetts, 'They are beating a child.' The neighbour pushed her complaint and the school mistress was charged.

Samuel Laycock. Author's collection

The boy was inspected and was found to have marks on the right temple, across his ear, on the right shoulder and on his right arm, with bruises from elbow to shoulder. There will always be those in control of children who abuse their status and power: this teacher did, and it cost her five shillings and costs if she wanted to avoid fourteen days in gaol. She paid.

The term 'clerical assault' was never found very often in the papers, but it was in 1886, because the Reverend Manwaring, Vicar of Stainton, was charged with assaulting nine-year-old George Jackson on 13 July. He did not act alone, because his housekeeper helped in the harsh punishment; all the boy had done was take a card into school with the words: 'No Primrose dames need apply here' on it. The reference was to the Primrose League, which had been founded in 1883 with the aims of spreading the Tory notions of 'upholding Queen and country and the Tory cause' and also 'To provide an effective voice to represent the interests of our members and to bring the experience of the leaders to bear on the conduct of public affairs for the common good.' That all sounds most innocuous, but the influential Lancashire poet, Samuel Laycock, wrote a satire against the League and the 'Primrose Dames' with these lines (in dialect):

Well they're at it again with their filth and their durt
*But it's **women** this time that are hondlin' the squirt...*

Laycock, who died in 1893, was immensely influential on popular working-class opinion. Clearly, this vicar had sympathies with the poet's opinions. But he was totally brutal in his punishment of the poor boy, who had no idea what the card was about. He told the housekeeper to tie the boy's legs together and then he thrashed him with a 'knob stick'.

One of the most stunning aspects of this story is that Manwaring had been convicted before, in 1877, for assaulting a little boy. We may sometimes tire of the modern concern for investigating the careers of those who work with children, but this sorry tale reminds us of what used to be. The vicar was fined £5. It seems utterly outrageous that he was not tried in a church court and disciplined by his peers.

CHAPTER 8

Outrage at Conisbrough
1855

A bottle with a lighted fusee attached to it was lying on the floor.

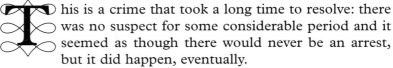his is a crime that took a long time to resolve: there was no suspect for some considerable period and it seemed as though there would never be an arrest, but it did happen, eventually.

In November 1855, Booth and Sons occupied Conisbrough Mills, manufacturing sickles and hooks, and Mr Booth lived with his wife very close to the mill buildings. At around three in the morning on 3 November, they woke up in fear. There was a loud crashing sound by a window and, as Mr Booth roused himself and got to his feet, he saw that the bedroom window was broken. Not only was there a ladder that had crashed against it, but a bottle with a lighted fusee was lying on the floor.

Booth lost no time in taking hold of his wife and dragging her out of the room: it was done in the nick of time, because as they got out, there was a powerful explosion behind them and the place quickly filled with sulphurous smoke. Other items in the room soon caught fire, including the bed and some clothes.

They were an elderly couple but had moved with alacrity and presence of mind; they did not run off either: with great fortitude they stayed around and began to put out the flames as the smoke cleared. They actually managed to stop the fire spreading, and by that time other people had been roused, several villagers arriving on the scene.

The hunt was on for the cowardly attackers. In Charles Dickens' periodical, *Household Narrative*, which took an interest in this provincial story, the report read, 'No traces of the perpetrator of this diabolical and cowardly outrage could be found.' That sentence was to resonate through the coming months as the frustration of there being no leads became apparent. The report went on to give an account of the damage done:

> *On examining the house it was discovered that the ceiling of the apartment in which the explosion took place was elevated two or three inches above its former position, as was also the ceiling of an adjacent closet; one of the walls was cracked, the bedroom door ... was forced three inches out of its position and the walls were deeply indented by the fragments of the stone bottle in which the explosive matter had been confined ...*

It is not hard to imagine what could have happened to the couple had they stayed in the room.

The obvious first line of thought was about employees, and whether there were any known who might have a grudge of some kind. But enquiries showed that Booth was a good and considerate employer who paid wages promptly and paid them in full. The couple were respected locally; but there some signs that two employees (called at the time 'hands') were not present on the evening of the bomb attack. Booth had heard someone running away after seeing the ladder smash the window. But nothing was found which we would now call scene of crime evidence.

The early and mid nineteenth century saw the growth of a great number of self-help groups among the landed classes: these were known as Societies for the Prosecution of Felons, and the local one, the Conisbrough Association, offered a reward of £50, to match the £50 put up by Booth himself and another £20 given by the Sheffield Trade Protection Society, offered to anyone who gave information leading to an arrest.

But there the frustration began. Reports in newspapers across the land continued to state that the man or men responsible had not been found. It was an ironical moment for such frustration because in the year after the event the Act was passed to make borough constabularies compulsory. A large number of towns and boroughs had been forming police forces since the 1830s but there had also been a long and bitter debate about where a proliferation of constabularies might lead – the chief fear being a 'police state' such as was said to be the case in France. But now, when this kind of crime was committed, and the reliance on well-meaning local and regional protection associations was seen as not quite good enough, and the constables of parishes also not equipped to become detectives, men like Booth must have longed for a police force.

Such a force would have used a network of information or even called in help from Scotland Yard, which had been happening in northern towns since the days of the Chartist fears in the 1830s. Six months after the first announcement of a reward, the government gave another £50, such was the desire to make some progress on this case.

Then, after eighteen months had passed, the *Leeds Mercury* had this news to announce: 'A watchman employed by Messrs Booth named Richard Swallow was apprehended on Friday (5 June) on suspicion of being concerned in the offence. On the same day he was examined by the West Riding Magistrates at Doncaster, but remanded.'

The paper had to remind readers what had happened over a year before, so long had been the wait for news.

The reason? The bland explanation given to the press was 'disagreement on trade matters'. It came down to what we would now call division of labour, and some workmen were not happy doing their part of the process of manufacture. Booth had not moved an inch on that and nothing had changed in the way he did things. Finally, there was a culprit and some sense of resolution. It was a very serious matter, and the offence was on the cusp between arson and attempted murder but the former won the day, along with related criminal damage. With a less capable lawyer, it could have been much worse for the man.

What is particularly interesting about the case is that the only gambit for over a year was to offer rewards. The reason was that the Societies for the Prosecution of Felons had come to believe that offering rewards for a 'grass' was the most effective way to flush out wrong-doers. That attitude was outmoded by the 1850s.

CHAPTER 9

Some Adventures of Inspector Winn
1858–1870

Wetherall identified him as the man he was searching for, and Winn at once seized him ...

There was no professional detective force in England until 1842, and that was only the start of it being formed in the Metropolitan Police. But as the century went on and regional forces were formed, there were small detective branches and plain clothes men across the land. It had formerly been common practice to ask Scotland Yard men to come out to the provinces when there was something that was beyond the resources of the regional force, such as Chartism or Luddites. There had been special constables and the police, of course, but when it came to the skills of detective work, specialists were needed.

The regional detectives in Victorian Britain are not well known, and the publications are few. One Manchester man, who was famous at the time, was Jerome Caminada, who worked mostly in Manchester and wrote his memoirs at the end of the century. He explained that drink and crime were inextricably mixed: 'Much of my work over twenty-seven years as a detective was aimed at closing down illegal beer houses and putting an end to criminal activities that happened on licensed premises.' He had something of a crusade in his later writings, asking the question: 'How come the worst criminals are the ones with the longest records?'

The new detectives in places like Doncaster and Sheffield had to practice what had been learned in London at the beginning: forming a string of contacts and snitches, using plain clothes disguises, and being as observant as we are asked to believe Sherlock Holmes was. They also had to learn how to cope with the more subtle types of crime – the non-violent ones that involved swindles, frauds and deception.

In the Doncaster area, the detective who stole the limelight in all kinds of contexts was Detective Officer Winn. He was based in Sheffield but often found himself at work in Doncaster and beyond. In 1858, he found himself on the tail of a forger who worked across south Yorkshire, going to horse fairs and passing dud cheques and forged notes. He had the same name as a very famous man of Victorian times – William Morris – and he was caught courtesy of the *Police Gazette*. This publication, still going well today, was originally called *Hue and Cry,* and was circulated across London at first and then further afield, with descriptions of wanted criminals, lists of army deserters and short accounts of crimes.

One day in April 1858, Detective Wetherall of Sheffield was on the hunt for Morris and when he went into one of the public houses where villains tended to congregate he saw a copy of the *Police Gazette* on a table. It couldn't have been a more significant clue: the publication was folded just as it had arrived, and there was a line drawing of Morris, visible. Wetherall knew that the best bet was that Morris had, through sheer crook's vanity, wanted to see how he was described in print.

It didn't take long to find out that Morris was lodging in a room upstairs and was in his room at that moment. Uttering false bank notes was a very serious offence: thirty years before this, it had been a hanging crime and even in the 1850s it had a likely sentence of many years penal servitude. In those days, when the police communication was still with whistles or feet, Wetherall had to run to the nearest police station for help. He knew that Officer Winn was a good man and he was there, so the two detectives were to get their man. They were soon entering the room where Morris was sitting. Wetherall identified him as the man he was searching for, and Winn at once seized him.

Detectives Winn and Wetherall knew that Morris had tried to drop a parcel in the corner of the room, and when they retrieved it, they found a roll of forged notes. Winn looked closely at them, and he knew that although they were cleverly done, with a correct watermark and excellent reproduction. But the officer's skilful eye could see that they were forged. Morris also had a bag of forged sovereigns on him, called 'jacks'.

The full story about Morris came out then: he had been a convict for many years and had returned on a ticket of leave. His life was transient and reckless, even though he had married recently – to a woman he had known only a short time.

Also in Sheffield, Winn collared another man who had been at work around Doncaster, and who had called at a butcher's saying he had several 'fat beasts' for sale. The normal price would have been around £20 but the man was asking for just £6. Clearly, this was a case of stolen cattle being shifted very quickly, and the rogue would have moved on elsewhere with a quick profit. The man was to gather his animals in the Sheffield Shambles and sell them there: Winn had learned that from a contact. The detective was soon there, in plain clothes, and he took the man in charge and had the cattle taken to the *Yellow Lion.*

George Winn was becoming a very smart professional by the early 1860s. In 1864, he was involved in one of his most high-profile cases, and one of Doncaster's most large scale burglaries in the nineteenth century. The crooks in the case were George Harris and George Perry from Huddersfield; they travelled across Yorkshire, 'casing' likely easy targets for burglary, and then worked as a team. They were adroit and cunning, and planned the work well, but on this occasion they met Winn and were taken into custody.

On 12 September in that year, the two men loitered on Christchurch Terrace by a house owned by a Miss Drabwell. She had gone away for a while to stay with her niece, but left her niece to look in and check the property when she could. But on the 20th the police were told that there had been 'an extensive burglary' there. Miss Drabwell was telegraphed and informed and she returned.

The thieves had broken into the house from the rear and then worked recklessly through the place, ransacking everything and going from room to room. Miss Drabwell was wealthy, and she kept a wine cellar. The thieves had discovered this and had a good time. Police found that several bottles had been drunk, two bottles of brandy had also been drunk, and the burglars had also smoked cigars there. As to the booty, the crooks went away with, the list was massive, including silver spoons, candlesticks, a silk mantle, silk jackets, a cashmere tablecloth and all kinds of silver items. They had also found and had taken thirty yards of satin and all kinds of jewellery.

But the burglars had a 'fence' called Charles Walker, and detectives kept an eye on him. Sure enough, at a shop belonging to a Mr Cash in Sheffield, a man who was working with the burglars went in and offered two seals. These had a crest on them, and Mr Cash was suspicious. Cash was used to helping police catch up with the rogues trying to unload their booty, so he asked the man to come back with more items and he would by them as a job lot. But Cash also told police, and who was waiting for the man in the afternoon? George Winn.

Charles Walker came to the shop, with the burglars behind; Walker had a bag under his coat, and Winn grabbed him. The other crooks ran away. But Walker spilled the beans under pressure and led Winn and officers to the lodging house where all the stolen goods were kept.

What is particularly interesting in the way the case ends, and the success of the hunt for the Doncaster burglars, is the Yorkshire detective network. The burglars returned to Huddersfield but descriptions had been sent on, and police were waiting for them. They were in the dock at Doncaster police court and sent on to Leeds Assizes, and from there to a long time behind bars.

We have a confirmation of Caminada's comments about drink and crime. When any kind of new or refurbished pub or 'eating house' was established, it was checked out. Obviously, known criminals would always be out to settle in a fresh den, and often with a 'legitimate' front. Winn was often man called in to help give these places a clean bill of health in terms of criminal potential. A typical example was the Alexandra Music Hall in Sheffield, where the magistrates were opposing a licence to the owner who was trying to import foreign wines.

Winn was called; he had clearly been to visit the place and also walked past it at different times of day, and he gave testimony to say that he had no grounds to be suspicious of the owner and staff.

This shows that the new detectives in the shires were powerful, influential men in some areas of urban life; the career of George Winn, Detective Officer, shows just how adaptable and resourceful these officers had to be, dealing both with the usual physical force side of policing and with white collar crime in that restless, pushy society which was opening up all kinds of new areas of crime as population expanded and industry diversified.

CHAPTER 10

He Shot to Kill
1864

The prisoner followed her, armed with a double-barrelled pistol ...

The first report of the fracas that almost led to two deaths was garbled and confused, such had been the chaos at a woman's house near Doncaster. It turned out to be a story of frustrated passion, a lover spurned and a gun that didn't work.

On 30 April 1864, a wheelwright and joiner from Brodsworth called William Wingfield had a serious disagreement with his housekeeper, Mary Birkenshaw. It was a matter that did not end in loud and angry words: Wingfield reached for a gun and set about shooting Mary. After the row, Mary went home to her mother's place, not far away. That could have been the end of it, but Wingfield followed her, armed with a double-barrelled pistol; he managed to get very near her, and was levelling the gun to fire when Mary acted spontaneously to defend herself, and raised an arm to the gun, jolting the barrel upwards; and the shot went harmlessly in the air.

Wingfield was determined, and in a terrible rage, but luckily for Mary, his gun was a very poor one, with faults. He fired at her again and this time there was a misfire. That was the cue for his rage to be incensed even more, as his supposed quick dealing with the object of his hatred had not happened. His next move was to grab a poker and beat her over the head with it.

Poor Mary screamed so loudly that a neighbour called Wilson heard, and came to help her. Wilson was heroic: he took hold of Wingfield and restrained him at first, but then he broke away and aimed the gun at the poor man who had come to help Mary, who was now severely injured. The gun was aimed at Wilson then, but again failed to fire. Fate was good that day to Wingfield, as the gun was useless: if it had worked, the wheelwright would almost certainly have been hanged.

This was the first account as the reporters heard it. What followed was to be a tragic tale of opposite wills and high emotion, saturated with violent hatred.

Wingfield was at last overpowered by more men who arrived in response to the noise and shouting. He was in custody, and then appeared at the West Riding Police Court on 2 May. Superintendent Astwood moved to remand his prisoner, and the solicitor for Wingfield asked for bail. There was no chance of that, and the magistrate refused the application.

At that point, there was no known reason why Wingfield had lost his head that day and brought out the gun. But more details emerged at the assizes. Wingfield had to wait a very long time for his trial, because the assizes for West Yorkshire were being transferred from York to Leeds (York was to be for the East Riding and North Riding). There was a long debate about this, and the usual bureaucratic process, so Wingfield was on remand in York until August, and then transferred to Leeds for trial. It was 17 August when he finally stood in the dock, charged with attempted murder. He was thirty-nine, and apparently from a well-respected family and a good background.

The core of the problem was that Wingfield had become bankrupt, and he was in such dire straits that Mary would have to leave his service. She left and stayed with her mother at Billingley, but they had become close and Wingfield expressed his affection for her: he wrote to her, and there appeared to be a possibility of their marrying at that point. Although marriage was a possibility, there was a strained relationship, and it was over the money: Wingfield owed her £14 – a large sum then. But in order to go through the official channels, Mary had to go to Doncaster to prove the debt, and she walked all the way there.

In court, the story was amplified: he had gone to her the next day and talked about their marrying and taking a house at Barnbugh, but Mary was truculent and ribbed him about a former girlfriend. It looks as though she had good reason for thinking that he had been seeing this Elizabeth again more recently. She said, 'Take the house, and live there with your Elizabeth then.' His reply begins to open up a complex relationship that makes this affair a 'crime of passion' in one respect. Wingfield replied: 'I would rather have you with half a dozen children than Elizabeth without any.'

It was a provoking refusal on Mary's part; she would not have him. His passions were roused, and his next words to her should have warned all concerned that there was likely to be trouble, because he said, 'If you do not have me, you will not have anyone else!' Then it all became much worse. He followed this with a threat: 'If I had been as well armed now as I was on the night when I came to see you, I don't know whether I should leave you alive. If I had known you were walking home last night, I would have been ready for you.'

This all happened at Mary's mother's home. The old lady was deaf and so she knew nothing about this dangerous talk. Their relationship was fiery to say the least. Wingfield followed Mary into another room and barred the door, then demanded a kiss. She refused, and he said, 'Then are you ready to die?'

He bolted the door of the parlour. She was a strong girl and grabbed his arm. There was a struggle and Wingfield went for his pistol in his pocket. That is when he fired at her and she warded off the shot. It was so close that it burned her hair. The first report had talked only of Mr Wilson coming, but there was also a woman called Sarah Shaw, and he fired at her but missed: then he set about her with a poker. He was striking Mary hard and she begged for mercy, saying she would marry him if he stopped the assault. It was at that point that she rushed out and Mr Wilson was rushing to the scene.

That second version, told at the assizes, explains so much about the confused motives involved. As to Wingfield, he was lucky to escape a conviction for attempted murder, and it was reduced to a lesser charge of shooting and wounding with intent to do grievous bodily harm. He received a sentence of ten years' penal servitude.

When the deaf mother had finally realised there was something wrong, Wingfield had replied, 'It's all right, I am just giving her a fright ... she will be all right in a few minutes.' That was when he was battering her head with the poker.

Penal servitude had been introduced just seven years before with the last of two Penal Servitude Acts, replacing transportation. The idea behind penal servitude, as one official statement said at the time, was to instil 'salutary dread'. Wingfield was in for a tough time. The *Correspondence on Convict Discipline* of 1843 had this account of penal servitude:

> *... we contemplate the necessity of subjecting every convict to successive stages of punishment, decreasing in rigour at each successive step until he reaches that ultimate stage of pardon ...*

We can only speculate as to what degree this regime would change a man like Wingfield – a terrible monster with a rage that would kill at a moment's instigation. He would have spent years sewing sacks, breaking stone and facing up to the dire consequences of his deadly temper. Hopefully, Mary found happiness with another man in the meantime – a man who would not want to shoot her or beat her on the head with a poker if she upset him.

CHAPTER 11

A Ten-Year-Old Tries to Kill 1866

He sat on the bank eating some bread and meat and watched their struggles ...

This is a story about a very nasty child who almost killed two other children. It is not Dickens' Artful Dodger, and there is no loveable rogue in this Doncaster tale which shocked the local community and made the legal professionals think very carefully about the punishment required.

In March 1866, Frederick Mason, just ten years old, was roaming around looking for mischief. He decided to entice two younger children away from their home in Rossington and put them through a terrible ordeal. He walked with them for a long time, so that he was nowhere near any other people, and then he began to beat them. He took a stick and struck them on the head and face; his victims were just five years and three years old, the eldest being a boy and the young one a girl.

After attacking them and seeming to enjoy their screams, he then took hold of them and threw them into the River Torne. Mason's behaviour defies explanation, particularly as he next sat on the bank eating some bread and meat and watched their struggles, then, unbelievably, responding to their screams and cries for help, he swore at them and then dragged them out so that he could hit them again.

The children had a second beating and were then thrown in the water again. The evil young creature then left them and ran away. Luck was on the side of the victims, and a passer-by called George Crosby heard their cries and ran to help. The boy, called Patrick, was close to the side of the bank and he pulled him to safety. The girl had her feet stuck in the mud and he could see that she was frantically just managing to keep her head above the water. Crosby rescued both and then, as he knew them, he took them to the hut where their father was. Both were not so far from death – the girl had convulsions afterwards and at the time was near death with hypothermia. It is virtually certain that she would have died if a policeman, Constable Cowan, had not been called and done some desperate first aid.

Cowan gave each child a little brandy, sent for a surgeon, and then had the girl's body rubbed with salt. When Mr Lister, the doctor, arrived he saw the dangerously weak condition of the girl and later testified that without Cowan's quick-thinking she would have died. The child was waivering between life and death for two days afterwards.

Mason was in court before justices Aldham and the Bench a few days later, and the case for the defence was that Mason was drunk and acted wildly and out of all character: he had, it was argued, drunk a pint of beer and eaten some mutton, but then met some other boys and shared a lot more beer with them followed by some gin. But the doctor, Lister, had been able to see him just after helping the victims because the police had brought him in and held him at the scene. He was sure that the boy was perfectly sober at that time. The police said that they had formed the same opinion. At the court hearing, the young criminal had stood impassive, saying nothing unless asked and then giving one-word replies.

Mason was committed for trial at the Leeds Assizes and there was an application for bail that was refused.

Events in recent times show that this kind of offence is always with us. In April 2009 there was a brutal attack by children on younger children near Doncaster, and of course, the Jamie Bulger case of 1993 brought complicated issues of children and violence into public debate. In the mid-Victorian years there was a great deal of fear in the streets because of gangs of children, and this was to be a common feature of life, perhaps peaking in the 1890s with the arrival of the word 'hooligan' and a gang culture in London and other major cities. But there was also, as this case shows, the problem of children on the loose, doing mischief and damage to property, in many areas of the land. Mason's parents knew nothing of his activities as he was left to roam, join gangs and generally do as he pleased.

At Leeds Justices Shee and Keating presided, and they had 103 people to attend to. Among the mass of adults waiting trial was young Mason. He was among five rapists, eleven killers, an arsonist, fourteen violent robbers and several other forgers and burglars. His case was listed in the causes – lists of charges – as 'attempt to drown'. At that time, the criminal law judged that a child between the years of seven and ten could not be guilty of a felony. The basic difference of felony and misdemeanour remained in English law until 1967, and the only aspect of a felony that was to change happened just four years after Mason's trial, when the forfeiture of estates and possessions of a felon was abolished.

One report noted that the law judged a child to be incapable of crime – an inaccurate statement, and something that showed the journalists could not cope with the repercussions of such a heinous crime. Technically, he was older than ten (he was ten years and nine months old) but this was disregarded. The report in the *Manchester Times* responded to the case with: 'One case in the calendar, however, was of a very peculiar character.' That understatement hints at the inability to explain matters.

In the language of the law, what could still happened was that the jury could find that Mason had committed a 'mischievous discretion' asserting that he knew what he was doing and that he knew it to be wrong. If they agreed on that, then a 'true bill' was formed against the child. This means that there was a case to answer in court. This happen, and the original charge was changed to grievous bodily harm. For an adult that would have had serious consequences and would have meant a long time in gaol doing hard labour. But for a ten-year-old child some other solution had to be found.

Mason returned to court a week later to hear the decision and this time, at Leeds Town Hall, he was given a sentence of fourteen days in prison, followed by five years in a reformatory. He was told directly: 'Had you been a man you would have been severely punished.'

There was one very odd feature of Mason's trial – that it happened in an adult court. In 1847 the Juvenile Offences Act ruled that young people under fourteen should be tried in a special court. Maybe Yorkshire had not caught up with legal changes in 1886, but a more likely explanation is that the authorities wished to instil a profound fear into the boy; after all, British criminal legislation has never quite applied to the real situations of gaols throughout history. Even in the 1980s there were some prisons in England in which young offenders mixed with old convicts on wings.

The short gaol term was to provide a shock: to instil fear into the lad. Two weeks in Armley with hardened offenders would have been intended to shock and horrify him regarding the consequences of breaking the law. As to the reformatory, that was another matter entirely. By the time Mason had done the unspeakably cruel acts of torment to the little children, there had been a reformative movement established across the country. This meant that there was a separate system of juvenile justice. Mason would have been absorbed into something lying between a young offenders' institution and a disciplined factory (as Borstal did not arrive until the early twentieth century).

The normal practice in dealing with juvenile crime was whipping and beating. One influential opposite line of thought was expressed by Mary Carpenter when she said it was necessary to make young offenders feel 'the brotherhood of man'. In the years c.1840–70 there was what one historian has called 'a preoccupation with the children of the dangerous classes'. In the case of young Frederick Mason, he had been left free to roam, to indulge in exerting his power of those weaker than himself, and then he had fallen in with a gang who were drinking and roaming the streets and fields. The parallels with modern ASBO culture are clear: the criminological answer lies in parental and community order and cohesion. Mason was left free to go either good or bad, and the parents were nowhere on the scene through the criminal process, except at the back, well out of sight, leaving everything to the officials.

We have no knowledge of Mason's future course of life, but his years in a reformatory would have meant long hours of hard work, vigilance over him at all times, and physical punishment if required. The same principles that were applying solitary confinement and forced time for 'inner reflection' were placed alongside work in order to change attitudes and hopefully to rehabilitate into society.

Reformatory schools were established in 1854, specifically for offenders under the age of sixteen; they were often beaten and punishments were severe, but we have to recall that around forty years before the Mason case, children of his age who committed a crime as serious as his would sometimes be hanged. In 1819 a girl called Hannah Bocking, aged sixteen, had been hanged at Derby and as late as 1831 a teenager had been hanged in Coventry for murdering her uncle. Extreme serious crime by teenagers was to remain a problem with regard to capital punishment even into the 1930s: in 1931 a sixteen-year-old was sentenced to death for murder, though he was later reprieved.

All we can say is that the name Frederick Mason does not occur in any Doncaster criminal context in the decades after this sentence given at Leeds to a young Sadist who clearly had no morality and a deep urge to inflict pain on the weak and helpless.

CHAPTER 12

A Wife Murder and a Knife Attack 1867

He took out his pocket knife and stabbed her in the neck.

One inescapable feature of Victorian crime is the very high level of violence against women. From the 1860s it became increasingly the case that the law was beginning to come down harder on men who murdered or badly injured women, particularly wives. The issues of the *Police News* are filled with dynamic illustrations of wife murderers. It was becoming something that was less tolerated. Earlier in the century, it was generally accepted in working-class communities that a husband would need to instil discipline by hand. But defences of provocation in the courts were increasingly more difficult to argue and maintain. As one historian has put it, provocation was being narrowed in definition, while intention was being broadened. In other words, provocation had to be much more serious than previously held, and there was more credence given to all kinds of reasons for going into a rage and intending to do harm or take life.

These two cases from the Doncaster area illustrate the two common crimes in this context: one is a vicious attack on a woman by an intruder and the other is the murder of a wife. The latter was an attack by a drunken husband who objected to his wife being similarly drunk, and the former was almost a murder – and just for a purse full of change.

Elizabeth Dawson was a widow who lived a lonely life away from others, in a quiet cottage between Hickleton and Barnburgh. On 9 February 1867, she was alone, and her dog barked. She went to the back door to see if anyone was there, and Charles Lister, a twenty-eight-year-old collier from Barnsley, was at the door. He asked if she wanted any manure

Knife attack in 1867. Author's collection

spreading on her land, and she said that she had already arranged for someone else to do that job. Lister was in a mood to make trouble, and he persisted in worrying the poor woman.

He pushed his luck and asked for some beer but Elizabeth tried to get rid of him. He apparently started talking and annoying her; the situation seems to be that he was building up the courage to act, and was in his own way, harassing and threatening his helpless victim. Of course, he had planned an attack and robbery anyway, so if he spoke and bluffed for a while, he could be certain that the woman was alone. He didn't like being asked to go. He lost his temper completely and grabbed her roughly, then asked where her money was. She was strong-minded enough to deny having any money but he was merciless and he hit her until she said that there was money in her purse. He took everything – coins to the value of about £4.

But this man was a cruel, heartless individual with a love of inflicting pain; he drew a razor and ran it across her throat, grazing the skin. She was then in total fear of her life and screamed for help. This goaded the man into further violence and he dragged her to some cellar steps and then threw her down – there were thirteen steps for her to fall.

His money was displayed to his future wife back home. Little did she know how he had come by it. But they were certainly never to marry. He was traced and arrested. Several people had seen him that day and some knew him. The judge at the Midland Assizes (held at Leeds after changes in 1864) stressed how serious this crime was and ordered Lister to do ten years of penal servitude.

The other story concerns a man known as Captain Slack around The Holmes, one of the poorest places, with mission churches and schools. When the story first broke, the press fastened onto the fact that Slack and his wife were both 'of intemperate habits' and that appears to have been the source of the man's murderous rages, this particular one proving to be the killing of his wife and his own ruin.

On 11 July, around six o'clock, Thomas Slack, aged forty, came home from a long drinking session; he found his wife, Ann, also drunk. They lived at The Holmes, in Wheatley. A little girl had been helping Ann do some housework, and she left just before Thomas appeared on the scene. The house had a kitchen and a front room, and later it was ascertained where exactly Slack struck – for he did strike, just minutes after coming home. He went into a rage when seeing her drunk: he took out his pocket knife and stabbed her in the neck. Ann staggered outside, screaming for help. She was bleeding heavily, and fell as she went outside, straight into the arms of a neighbour who had rushed to the spot.

The woman who first held the dying woman was Hannah Slack (aunt by marriage to the prisoner), and she left Ann breathing her last, with another woman before going inside and confronting the man. Hannah found him in the front room, sitting on a sofa with his hand in his pocket and she said: 'You have murdered your wife!' Slack answered: 'I have not seen her, where is she?' But the drunk strangely then added: 'Oh is she dead? She was my best friend...I'm very sorry.'

Hannah Slack now emerges as the heroine in the tale. The hand in his pocket grasped his knife and he said that he was going to take his own life. Hannah restrained him and shouted for help. It was very risky for her to have gone in there alone, in the first place. The other neighbours around responded and finally came to her assistance. Slack was grabbed and held, and a short time after the police arrived, led by Superintendent Astwood, who arrested Slack and took him away. He was charged with murder but he was sober enough to say that it was not so, because he was in drink. That was significant, because at court he stood indicted on charges of both murder and manslaughter.

The definition of murder needs to be placed at this point in the sad story: a murder is a killing which is done 'with malice aforethought' – there has to be a *mens rea* – an aim to kill – and then the *actus reus* – the deed done which would lead to the taking of life. The two Latin terms are crucially important. Slack had immediately thought that his drunkenness would be a defence and would pre-empt a murder charge. He was wrong.

Dr Charles Fenton gave medical evidence, saying he arrived on the scene about forty-five minutes after the deadly attack. He found a wound two inches long on Ann's neck; this was close to the left ear and death had been caused by the piercing of the carotid artery.

It was clear from this that the knife wound had caused the death.

It was looking bleak for Slack. His defence, Mr Price QC, straightaway introduced the notion of provocation, saying: 'I have known and worked with the family for several years... Mr Slack is a good and kind husband. The deceased was very unkind and provoking in every sense of the word. She did not bear a good character.'

Price then launched into the high drama of the plea aimed at the jury, insisting that this had not been wilful murder. He said, cleverly, 'that the law was bound to lay down general principles, but the application of these principles lay with the jury...' In other words, he was angling for the wilful murder to be dropped by reason of severe provocation. The argument was that Price had suffered long and hard over the years, worthily trying to bring this fallen woman back to habits of sobriety.

But Hannah Slack's testimony was crucially important. Slack had some barges on the River Don, hence his nickname, and Hannah pointed out that he was often away from home; their marriage was a very unhappy one, she said. Then she described how she had seen both of them very drunk on that fateful evening. After the killing, but before Hannah had known, she saw Slack walking along the garden and he 'doubled up his hands and ruffled his hair in quite a delirious manner'.

Price was stretching all sinews and brain cells to paint a good picture of Slack. He cross-examined Hannah and she explained: 'He has had to call me up dozens of times when he could not get deceased to bed because she was so drunk... I have often seen men come to the house when he has been away.' The tale of their life together was depressing. Hannah pointed out that when the Slacks were first married they had a well-furnished house. Drink had led Ann to pawn absolutely everything for beer or gin-money, and Hannah pointed out that there was not even a blanket in the house to put over the deceased body.

It was seeming that the man had been driven to distraction, and the presiding judge, Mr Justice Lowe, asked Price if he intended to set up an insanity defence. The answer was no: he was keeping to the provocation appeal.

The Slacks had been married for ten years, but for the last six months the decline had been extreme. Hannah said that Slack had been going to Sheffield almost every day in that period, and coming home drunk, finding yet more items pawned and both of them heading for complete destitution.

There was no doubt about the version of events given at the first statement of the events: Mary Humphrey, a neighbour, testified that she had held Ann as she died, and confirmed that she was very intoxicated. Thomas Bramworth, another neighbour, came to the scene and he recalled saying: 'Slack, whatever have you done?' and the man had replied:

'Do save her life and take mine ... she was the best friend I had!'

Superintendent Astwood confirmed that Slack had denied murder when in custody in Doncaster. So what was the situation at that point? It was that Slack was being painted for the jury as a man distracted, one who although he had a severe drink problem himself, he was possibly stretched to mental instability all because of his wife. In other words, there was no talk of his actions causing the relationship to deteriorate and no account of his failure to act with regard to the financial worries – all he had done was spend more.

The jury found Slack guilty of manslaughter. But the judge had a shock in store for Slack, and for Price, his barrister.

The judge summed up with an oblique and vague reference to potential human understanding of Slack's situation. He said: 'I am quite sure that both the jury and myself would gladly give effect to any circumstances if they could do so consistently with their duty.' But there was a word from his mouth that had a tone of foreboding for Slack: he said 'But ...' His final words were:

The jury has taken a very merciful view of this case. There was no doubt that it was a moral murder, although legally manslaughter. If any circumstances should arise, either as regarded his health or otherwise, they must be the subject of an application to a higher authority. But I feel it right, for an offence of this kind, although committed in a moment of drunkenness and repented afterwards, to have a sentence of twenty years' penal servitude.

This was a bombshell in the court. The sentence was, in those times, virtually a sentence to a future of a 'living death'. Slack would enter a limbo in which he would move from hard labour and fearful discipline into such a drain of his self-identity that should he live to the age of sixty and complete the sentence, he would be a broken man.

Through the whole trial, Slack had been in a posture of prayer and was indeed heard to mumble words. He had been given permission to sit, as he was not well. But that modicum of consideration was something that must have misled all present with regard to the nature of this judge. In the end, a life had been taken with intent. The judge knew that, and that is what he meant by 'moral murder'. He found a way to defeat and deflect the jury's decision into something that he personally knew was justice.

A woman in the low condition of the poor deceased, however aggressive and difficult, deserved a husband who would try to help, try to change things for the better – not a man who would take her life in a drunken rage.

CHAPTER 13

The Death of John Lee
1882

One of the other men came and kicked him three or four times on the head.

This is a heart-rending story of a pointless death, a killing done in the crazed heat of revenge. It is a murder carried out by a gang of cowards, perpetrated because one of them was insulted in a pub disagreement. It could be any one of thousands of such horrible crimes – a man kicked and beaten to death outside a

The attack at the Salutation Inn. Vicki Schofield

BRUTAL MURDER AT DONCASTER.

A brutal murder was committed in Doncaster about half-past eleven o'clock on Thursday night. It appears that a farmer named John Lee, of High Ellers, went to the Salutation Hotel about half-past ten, and there met with two or three stud grooms, who had come with horses to the Agricultural Show. One of them, named John Hodgson, who is groom to the Stand Stud Company at Manchester, began arguing with Lee about the judging; and finally the conversation turned to "chaffing," when Hodgson told Lee he had got a "magpie face," and asked him to speak plainly. Lee was much annoyed at this, and watching his opportunity, got up and struck Hodgson in the face, fetching blood. The landlord, Mr. J. M. Axe, intervened, and at eleven o'clock the ___ ___

Fearing that the men would wait for Mr. Lee, the landlord sent for a cab to take him home. When the cab arrived, the men were standing near the house, one man being behind a pillar. They asked the cabman who he had come for, and, on being told, said, "That's the man we want." Mr. Axe opened the door, and letting Lee out closed it, and went back. Directly Lee got to the door, the man standing behind the pillar struck him several times and knocked him down. One of the other men came forward and kicked him three or four times on the head, whilst another man said—"If you can't do it, I can." The cabman's horse was startled, and bolted, and the cabman had to attend to it. Mr. Axe, hearing the thump at the door, went out and found Lee laid on his back. Hodgson, Burke, and two or three other men were there. He said, "I am afraid you have killed him," to which they made no reply. The deceased was carried into the house, and was then dead. One of the men, named Burke, groom to Mr. Lett, of York, helped to carry him in, and seemed very anxious about the man's condition. Dr. Clarke and the police were sent for. An officer named Dawson was on the other side of the road when the attack took place. The men then went away, but Hodgson, Burke, and two other men have since been apprehended. An inquest was opened yesterday afternoon by Mr. Atkinson, the Borough Coroner, and adjourned until Monday, at two o'clock, after the evidence of Mr. Axe and the cabman, James Cooke, had been taken.

'Brutal Murder at Doncaster', from The Times. The Times

pub. But this one happened in Doncaster, and it happened outside the *Salutation Hotel*. As remarked previously, the place was linked to all kinds of suspicious deaths at this time. Some of those deaths were not necessarily suspicious, but this one –

the murder of a farmer – was more than suspicious, it was ruthless, heinous and thoroughly despicable.

The background for these events was the Doncaster market, specifically the fat-stock and horse market. Stock was brought in mainly from a twenty-mile radius of the town, but farther away as well, as this story will show. The grooms of big horse outfits would be around the place, mixing with farmers and labourers. The writer Fred Archer in his book, *Brother to the Ox,* described Doncaster market around 1900 in this way: 'The streets were crowded with farm chaps seeking new masters, and all were dressed in breeches and leggings.' The fairs were often places where there was trouble. One old song often sang at this time and in the area had the lines, *'For I'm barn to beggin' and alter mi way/ I'm gerrin sa thin and sa pale/ for ah'll nivver get fourteen days na more/ I'Wakefield Jail.'*

The trouble began when John Lee, a farmer from High Ellers, went to the pub and met three stud grooms who had come to the agricultural show. With one of these in particular, a man called John Hodgson, he started a heated argument about the nature of the judging at the show. Hodgson, who worked for a Manchester firm called the Stand Stud Company, began to tease Lee, and insulted him. He called him a 'magpie face' and told him to say what he meant. By 'magpie' Hodgson was most likely jibing about the insincerity of Lee – that he was double-talking – because magpies were associated with dishonesty, as in these lines from an eighteenth century handbook, quoted in Johnson's *Dictionary*:

> *Dissimulation is expressed by a lady wearing a vizard of two faces, in her right hand a magpie, which Spenser described looking through a lattice …*

In the language of the twenty-first century, Hodgson was saying that Lee was two-faced and never giving a straight answer. It was the beginning of a quarrel that would escalate out of all proportion. Lee cracked Hodgson across the face and the man had a bloody nose.

Hodgson was rankling with thoughts of a violent response to this public insult, and only the intervention of the landlord,

Joseph Axe, protected Lee from vengeance. It was clear that Hodgson would not act alone: he had his bunch of friends, other grooms, who made it clear that they would back him. The landlord wisely formed a protective buffer zone between Lee and the gang, and at closing time he kept the farmer back and ordered a cab for him, thinking that would avoid any nasty later events outside.

He was wrong. After closing time, Hodgson and his cronies loitered outside, awaiting their prey. When the cab arrived, they were outside, and Hodgson was behind a pillar. The men outside saw the cab arrive and asked the cabman, James Cooke, who he had come to collect. When he said it was Lee, Hodgson said, 'That's the man we want!' The door was opened and Lee walked out. As soon as he was visible, Hodgson rushed at him and knocked him down; one of the other men came and kicked him three or four times on the head. At that point there was a very important sentence spoken by someone else, whose identity was later discovered. He said, in the hearing of the cabman, 'If you can't do it, I can.' That seems to imply that they meant to kill him. The words 'do it' must have referred to something more than a beating-up and a kicking because they had already achieved that.

The cabman was distracted because his horse was playing up at the noise, but he still heard things that would be his testimony in court. But in the fracas, one man had banged against the pub door and the landlord came out to see what was happening. He saw Lee on the floor and tried to help. He was sitting up, bleeding from his face.

There was an inquest, chaired by the Borough Coroner, Mr Atkinson, which sat after an initial adjournment. The principal figures in the attack, Hodgson and Burke, had been apprehended. There were members of Lee's family present of course, and also the cabman, Cooke. Mr Rollett and Mr Verity represented the deceased family. Cooke identified Hodgson as the man who had come out of the shadows first and attacked Lee; he was sure that Lee was taken by surprise and given several hard blows. He went down and his head cracked the pavement. Cooke had been taken to the Doncaster police cells to see if he could pick out the other attackers. He thought the man in question might be Burke, but was not completely sure. In terms of identifying the man, he said that the landlord had said that the attacker who kicked Lee had been wearing knee-breeches. This is exactly how Fred Archer described a groom in his memoir, referred to earlier: 'Next to Mary sat Ernest Gill, a groom wearing very loud check riding breeches, and looking altogether out of place in this soberly clad community.' So the grooms stood out, they were a group with a certain pride and supportive mentality if there was trouble – and they liked a tipple.

Cooke said he cried out, 'Don't kick the man like that ... give him a chance!' It was confirmed that Hodgson never came face to face with his victim, but hit him on the side of the head. Cooke said that he could see there was going to be a fight but that everything happened so quickly he could do nothing except shout, and then his horse took fright. He said, 'Mr Lee was struck before he had moved a yard away from the pub door.'

Cooke was pressed for more, but did not respond, and a police officer, James Dawson, was over the road. He said he had been on duty in Regent's Square and that some people had told him there was trouble. Dawson, it has to be said, must take some blame. His testimony was that he saw the pub door open and then heard some thuds, hollow sounds. He then realised there was an attack and that someone on the ground was being kicked. The officer then added that Axe, the landlord, had come out and they sat Mr Lee up in a sitting position. Oddly, Axe told the constable that no one had attacked him – which is contradictory to his first statement that he told the attackers they had killed him.

A crowd had gathered after Lee was sat up; Dawson called for brandy and tried to give some to Lee, but he saw that none of this went down his throat and it was then that he saw how serious the man's condition was. He said, 'I told Mr Axe we had better carry him into the house and asked some of the men to help. It did not occur to me to take hold of any of the men ...' Axe had seen that Lee had died and said so. It was then that he said, 'You have killed him.' Dawson then asked

Axe and Cooke for some names. Burke was named, and it was known that he worked for a Mr Lett. But he and another constable, called Leaning, later went to the showground and arrested Hodgson and Burke. Two others, called Fox and Kelly, were later arrested.

Before the magistrates, after a coroner's decision of 'wilful murder by John Hodgson and other person or persons unknown,' Kelly, a groom from Darlington, stood in the witness box and said that he and others had been to a pub called the *Dolphin* after going to the theatre, and had then walked on to the *Salutation*, where he met Hodgson, and saw that there was a crowd gathered. He said, 'Hello John, what's the matter with thee?'

Hodgson replied, 'Not much. A man inside hit me in the face. We were having a bit of a chaff together and I happened to say there was something of the magpie in his face…when he came across he struck me in the face.'

Hodgson and Burke had been charged with manslaughter, and they were remanded to appear at the West Riding Assizes in Leeds before Mr Justice Cave. There, the witness testimonies were heard again, and some details came out about the initial altercation, with one man saying that Hodgson had 'twitted Lee about his defective pronunciation' – so the 'chaffing' appears to have had more than one cause of disagreement.

The medical evidence stated that Lee had died from a rupture of the brain, and there had been contusions on the head; this was said by Kelly, and both Fox and Kelly were considered to be 'tainted' witnesses by Hodgson's defence counsel. A man called Charles Lee Clare from Manchester gave a strong, positive character witness statement for Hodgson, saying that he had never been in trouble before. Hodgson had worked for several years for Lord Derby, and he had earned very good money.

In the end, it came down to the immediate cause of death – was it from the blows of Hodgson or the kicks of Burke? The latter had by this time been identified as the man who kicked Lee on the ground. The jury decided that Burke's kicks were the deadly action in that night of confusion and rage. William

Burke, aged twenty-six, was guilty of manslaughter. His sentence was deferred to a later date, but his rage cost him five years of penal servitude.

On the night of the killing, it has to be said that it is highly likely that first of all no passers-by wanted to be involved in what must have seemed like one more drunken brawl (a regular event) and the police officer, Dawson, possibly saw most of the stages of the attack but was slow to act and kept clear until there seemed to be a resolution. But we have to ask why he did not detain anyone after the fact of the man's death was verified.

CHAPTER 14

Magistrates and Juveniles
1889

There would not be one of them who not have given her a child's whipping.

In January 1889, a minor episode of shoplifting in Doncaster reached the national newspapers and caused a lengthy debate. That may have been unusual for a Doncaster story, but the subject was certainly nothing new. The general public had been well informed about 'rings' of child thieves, most famously by Charles Dickens in *Oliver Twist* back in 1838; and after that year there had been a constant fear of child criminals. The main statutory measures against the problem had been the

Beer Shop, showing children, from Alan Bott's Our Fathers (1902). Author's collection

establishment of the reformatories in the 1850s. That had been one way of dealing with juvenile crime – take the little villains away from home and work them into submission!

These tough measures had not really addressed the heart of the problem. If we accept that in the history of crime, drink and poverty have always been causal factors, then that was central to the Victorians, and they had those problems in the absolute extreme. The massive demographic shift of labour into the new towns after the Enclosure Acts (accelerated after 1801), and the proliferation of the factories and mills, had created a general need for child labour, and education had been slow to develop as a remedial measure – something to make childhood happy and hopefully imaginative. But that the universal influence of beer shops and the habit of drinking gin at all times was a formative tendency in making poverty a massive social issue.

The result was that the late Victorian years had new debates about children and the law. One of the commonest features of this was the context of what we now try to deal with in issuing the ASBO: children left out to roam, create trouble and fend for themselves.

This was the case in Doncaster at this time, and the story that reached the dignified pages of *The Times* was one featuring two children: a brother and sister called Margaret and Daniel Fell. They went on a stealing spree in Doncaster one day and stole £2 from a confectioner in Hall Gate called Miss Brooks. That was quite a lot of money, but matters were more serious when it was found that they had raided several other shops, averaging a few pounds in cash from each one.

The boy was ten and the girl seven; they had been taught to steal by a mysterious child called Harker, and of her there is nothing else known but her name. Margaret and Daniel took their booty and met another child, then all three decided to have a day out in Lincoln. There, they appear to have spent their takings, and not stolen anything; they then went for a number of rides on the trams, and it was while on one of these that a driver became suspicious and called the police.

At the Doncaster Police Court, the children faced their punishment. The Chief Constable, Isaac Gregory, recounted the events of the day of the spree, and he said that their parents, 'Had a good deal of trouble with these children.' He told a familiar story: that the children were never supervised and the parents never had an idea where they were; he said they were, 'allowed to go prowling about at night.' It is surely unusual that the Chief Constable was there to speak. It is hardly a job for the senior police officer. Perhaps that tells us that this case was merely one of many similar ones and that juvenile crime was reaching mammoth proportions.

That appears to be the case when we consider the response to this crime. But what caused the heated response was the punishment. In Doncaster, the magistrate ordered Daniel Fell to receive 'six strokes from the birch rod', whereas Margaret received no punishment and was too young to be sent to a reformatory. The only additional action taken was that the parents (who bothered to turn up) were admonished and told to take better care of their children in future. A correspondent to *The Times* picked up the story and wrote:

'The reason why the real thief was dismissed scot-free and her less guilty brother whipped was, of course, not the one given by the magistrates ... Had the girl been the child of one of the magistrates, there probably was not one of them who, when he got home, would not have given her a child's whipping.'

The author of the letter was the Earl of Meath, and he was really making a point about the reformatories and the age at which young offenders could be sent to one of those institutions. From 1854 the ruling had been that only girls under the age of sixteen could be sent to a reformatory. For children such as Daniel and Margaret, the punishment was whipping and a caution. In earlier times, public humiliation had been the punishment, with the use of stocks and pillory, but in these supposedly more enlightened times, a beating was considered to be a civilised measure. As early as 1816 there had been a parliamentary committee to investigate juvenile crime, but little was done; children could still be sent to prisons along with adults of course, and this continued until the year following this hearing in Doncaster. Just thirteen years after these Doncaster children were in court – in 1902 – the first Borstal was established.

But the issue of fair punishment was still there at the time. The Earl of Meath was answered by 'a Board Master', anonymously. He argued that, 'I must join issue with him in his suggested remedy – viz., the substitution of the birch for the cane.' The schoolmaster was worried about the repercussions, saying of the birch, 'That instrument has hitherto been looked upon only as an adjunct to police courts, and its introduction into schools would, I fear, stir up popular clamour.'

In other words, the middle-class establishment figures, those with power to apply corporal punishment, had their limits and also their choices of suitable items of torture. It was all about a moral panic in 1889. The teacher wanted tough measures, and his statement on that opens up an insight into the depth of the public fear: 'The young men composing these bands of desperate, defiant law-breakers were shown at school what a fine thing it was to cheek the master, who could be summoned if he presumed to do aught but meekly endure it; and the disregard of the rule increased with their growth.'

The two Doncaster children lived at a time when there were serious social problems with gangs of youngsters, and their shoplifting spree opened up a 'can of worms'. The 1880s and 1890s saw a massive increase in the larger, more threatening groups such as the Regents Park Gang and, in Liverpool, the High Rip Gang. The fact that a day of shoplifting could lead to these significant national discussions is very informative about the state of affairs in this respect. The corporal punishment regime throughout society was not working; flogging in the armed forces was stopped only a few years before this case – in 1881 – and social historians have shown that corporal punishment within the family and in school continued until the 1960s in many areas.

Even sixty years later there were still debates and disagreements about juvenile crime, and in a sense this never goes away. In Liverpool, between 1949 and 1953, an experimental scheme involving visits by police to 39,000 homes, schools, youth clubs and churches showed a considerable achievement in understanding the causes of such crime, but there is never an easy solution. In the Doncaster case, the everyday incident of the shopping spree highlighted the timeless issue of what the results of freedom given to children might be. The Victorian mindset never quite understood, as Charles Dickens did so well, that a repressive education with no encouragement to the imagination in the classroom, creates rebels.

CHAPTER 15

The Baccarat Scandal 1890

The scandal that followed was colossal. Not only in England, but abroad, the press teemed with it ...

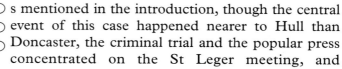s mentioned in the introduction, though the central event of this case happened nearer to Hull than Doncaster, the criminal trial and the popular press concentrated on the St Leger meeting, and Doncaster was tainted with the case. At the trial, the barrister Sir Edward Clarke, defending the plaintiff, told the world that Tranby Croft 'was near Doncaster'. The son of the Archbishop of Canterbury, EF Benson, wrote that, 'Tranby Croft, near Doncaster' was where this all took place. As far as the readers of this great law case were concerned, the 'Baccarat Scandal' was a Doncaster races affair.

Sir William Gordon-Cumming was a very successful soldier in 1890; at just forty-two years old he was a personal friend of the Prince of Wales, and he had won distinction and awards in the 1879 Zulu War, and in several famous battles in the Egyptian campaigns of the early 1880s. But in a house party in 1890 he was accused of cheating at cards and his life was, in many ways, totally ruined.

This scandal – beginning with a group of friends enjoying some time together at the Doncaster St Leger meeting – led to one of the most celebrated defamation cases in British legal history, with Lord Coleridge presiding. Sir William brought an action for slander against four defendants who had accused the baronet of cheating. As the party enjoyed themselves as guests of the shipping magnate Sir Arthur Wilson at Tranby Croft, Anlaby, a game of baccarat was arranged. The group included the Prince of Wales (the future King Edward VII), and most were good friends of him and of the family. In fact,

Sir William Gordon-Cummings.
Author's collection

Sir William did not know the Wilsons well at all, and had stayed there just once before, five years earlier, again for the races.

Baccarat involves a banker and two pairs of players. There is no real skill involved, and the aim is to gather cards and replace cards, trying to reach a score of eight or nine. The fact is that this was not high-level gambling, and leather tokens were used to limit the sums risked. But after a makeshift table had been put in place, the game began, and the son of the magnate, AS Wilson, reported to others that he had seen Sir William cheating. By the end of the night, there were five people who were all of the opinion that he had cheated. Nothing was said, but the next night, with a different table, the soldier was closely watched again, although at the trial it was never stated that the accusers planned to observe their alleged cheat. However, it seems highly likely that they did.

EF Benson expressed the uneasy and delicate nature of this accusation when he wrote: 'A party of friends and of guests was to sit down to a cheery little game of cards and all the time there would be going on this grim piece of criminal investigation...'

Benson observes that, '...detective work among friends appeared...a prohibitively ugly business'. The essence of the cheat was that Sir William, with the Prince of Wales as the banker, added more to his stake if he had a good card, and withdrew his stake, or some of it, if he had a bad card. The observers told the other officer present, General Owen Williams, of their suspicions, and it was decided that the Prince should be told.

Prince Edward made a decision that was to cause all kinds of complications later in court. He thought that it would be wise if Sir William signed a solemn oath not to gamble at cards ever again. The Prince and his friend had a quiet word and the paper was signed. Sir William asserted that he was totally innocent, but signed the paper to avoid a scene. There was a tacit agreement that no one would mention what had happened to anyone else outside that circle. Of course, someone did.

Benson wrote that, 'The scandal that followed was colossal. Not only in England but abroad the press teemed with it.' The day after the card game, Sir William was seen at Doncaster races, looking 'anxious and depressed, and the rest of the party, including the Prince, had no converse with him'. It was said by some that no one broke the story and that the press and others investigated the cause of this strained social division and found out the truth. But whatever the facts, the following sensation made the Prince the centre of the scandal. He was cartooned and satirised everywhere. He was a pleasure-loving and sporting type, with a love of manly pursuits and female companions. He travelled widely and was seen with all kinds of important celebrities and dignitaries in his company. But now it seemed that he was a terrible gambler and had participated in nothing short of an orgy of iniquity.

What had actually happened was that a card game had been played for very small stakes (small in terms of the wealthy participants) and one of the Prince's closest friends was a 'cad' and no gentleman.

In fact, it is almost certain that there had been a threat to publicly shame the Lieutenant General by proclaiming him a cheat at the Doncaster races the next day, and we have to wonder if that was the cause of his observed melancholy that second day. But fate had stepped in: there was a death in the Wilson family, and the normal course of the leisure weekend was interrupted. But the essence of the case as far as the Prince was concerned was that he had to appear in the witness box. The prince had not believed his friend to be guilty, but in asking him to sign the paper, that was interpreted as a sign of guilt. What was intended by Sir William to protect the Prince had not worked out because of a 'leak' from the ten people at Tranby Croft who knew of the supposed cheating.

If there had been any public announcement or accusation made in front of the gentlemen of the press, it would have been most unseemly, given the manners around the Doncaster St Leger meeting. One journalist, Robert Watson, was at the St Leger meeting just six years after this affair, and he wrote:

A post-horn here and there heralded the approach of a party anxious to be noticed. There was nothing falsely suggestive in the character of the crowd, no ribaldry, coarse banter, screaming, hysterical laughter or profane language, at least not distinct enough to offend the ears...At Doncaster, buffoonery was absent...I looked in vain for a drunken man, and worse still, a drunken woman...

A myth grew in the popular press that the Prince was an inveterate gambler and that he took gambling counters with him everywhere he travelled, and forced people to join in his gambling sprees. Of course, the fact that the party was there for the St Leger did not help matters. To make matters worse, Sir William had breached army regulations. In June 1891, the Secretary of State for War was asked if he intended to act against Sir William for the breach. The military ruling stated: 'Every commissioned officer of Her Majesty's service, whose character and conduct as an officer and a gentleman had been publicly impugned, must submit the case within a reasonable time to his Commanding Officer or other competent military authority for investigation.' It was decided to do nothing because Sir William's conduct at the time convinced superiors that he did all he could not to make the conduct 'public'.

ARTHUR WILSON DEAD.

Steamship Owner Worth $15,000,000— Card Scandal at Tranby Croft.

News was received in this city by cable yesterday of the death of Arthur Wilson of Tranby Croft, near Hull, England, of general debility, in his seventy-fifth year. He was the Chairman of Thomas Wilson Sons & Co., Limited, which operated lines of steamships to all parts of the world, and was considered to be the wealthiest ship owner in the world. Where other companies in England went bankrupt the Wilson lines paid dividends on their savings, and were operated on the most economical basis. The liners are all painted green with red funnels and black tops, and go to Pier 50 North River in this city.

Arthur Wilson was the father of Muriel Wilson, the English beauty, who is still unmarried. It was at his seat, Tranby Croft, several year ago, that King Edward, then Prince of Wales, detected Sir William Gordon Cumming, Bart, cheating at cards, and a scandal ensued, which ended in the law courts, and practically ended the social aspirations of Mrs. Arthur Wilson. Charles Wilson, the eldest brother of Arthur, was created a peer by King Edward under the title of Lord Nunburnham, and died a year ago. The scandal at Tranby Croft had a seri-

'Arthur Wilson Dead', from the New York Times. *Even at his death, the Baccarat Scandal was mentioned in the shipping magnate's obituary.*

All this means that the Prince took a great deal of criticism, and indeed, libel. But he could do nothing in response. Our best insight into his predicament comes from his meeting with the Archbishop of Canterbury. They met at Marlborough House and he gave his reaction to the whole affair; this was passed on to AC Benson by the Archbishop, and letters from the Prince to the Archbishop have survived. Edward said, according to Benson:

'They say that I carry about counters, as a Turk carries his prayer carpet ... but the reason why I carry counters is to check high play. High sums are easily named but these counters range from five shillings to five pounds ...' He also responded to the press accusation that Wilson at Tranby Croft objected to anyone playing cards in his home, but had been dominated by the arrogant Prince. Benson said, 'He had been absolutely unaware at the time that Mr Wilson had any objection to games of cards being played in his house, and when he had enquired into it he found it to be untrue.'

Edward wrote to the Archbishop: 'I have a horror of gambling and should always do my utmost to discourage others who have an inclination for it, as I consider that gambling, like intemperance, is one of the greatest curses which a country can be inflicted with.' He had to bear a deluge

The King's Entrance at Doncaster Racecourse. By kind permission of Doncaster MBC, Ref: AB/RACE/69

of attacks in the press everywhere, reading this kind of account of his activities in the affair (from the *Dundee Advertiser*): 'It should be remembered that among the company present at this vulgar house and taking part in or silently acquiescing in this gamblers' orgy were Lord and Lady Coventry, General Sir Owen Williams, the Earl of Craven, Mr Reuben Sassoon, Lady Brougham … and Mr Christopher Sykes …' One commentator at the time summed up the effect of this: 'If the Prince himself had been detected cheating he could not have been more savagely sentenced.'

One simple fact emerged at trial which explains some of the reactions in the press. As they were mostly speaking for the common man, as it were, the sum that the soldier had won – £225 – was a very large amount by working-class standards. That must have had some impact on popular opinion.

Sir William had to resign from the Army, and of course, his reputation was ruined. But it had not been a criminal trial – that would have entailed a prosecution under the Gaming Act of 1845, section 17. It was a civil court, and it took the jury only ten minutes to decide in favour of the defendants – so Sir William was thought of as a cheat by the country generally. The whole sorry business entered popular culture. In 1925, the popular magazine, *Truth*, carried a large coloured illustration of the baccarat party, conveying an atmosphere somewhere between a 'gambling orgy' and drunken revelry.

There were also legal repercussions, and in a book published in 1937, *The Royal Baccarat Scandal*, by Sir Michael Havers, Edward Grayson and Peter Shankland, issues of procedural errors were discussed, including the fact that the accusers in Tranby Croft were under no obligation to say any more than they thought the cheating had occurred at a specific time and place. Such niceties would not have worried Sir William at all – but his saga in the court had created a major case to trouble future law students trying to understand concepts of defamation.

CHAPTER 16

Suffragette Problems
1913

Her particular intention was to burn down every empty building that she saw ...

On 2 June 1913, seventy-two-year-old Mary Beecroft, a caretaker at Westfield House, Balby, woke up, disturbed by a noise at the house. A window had been broken and she went to investigate. She certainly showed some bravery, getting up, lighting a candle and walking towards the sound, shouting out to ask who was there. Mary must have had a shock when she heard a reply. A voice said, from downstairs, 'We are only Suffragettes and doing no harm.'

The intruders actually apologised. Mary must have been expecting some determined local thugs, villains thinking that the house was empty and there might be something worth taking. But the forceful Mary told the Suffragettes to get out and then tried to blow a whistle, but failed to attract any passing policeman or helpful citizen until early the next morning when a sergeant came and investigated. He must have thought he was dealing with rank, bungling amateurs when he found materials in the garden that clearly pointed towards an intended arson; his surprise must have been unbounded when he also found a name: that of Miss Key Jones. Suffragettes or not, this was a serious case. If Mary had not stirred, she may have been a victim of their burning down of the house. Arson often brings a homicide along with it.

The Key Jones in question was Violet Key Jones, a woman who had been given the responsibility of creating problems for the authorities down the side of Yorkshire, stretching from Doncaster to York. She had a base in Doncaster and had helpmates, including an intriguing character called Harry

Johnson, who had been there that night in Balby, ready to set the place alight. Violet was a daughter of a rich family in the York area; her uncle was at Water Fulford Hall at that time, with his family. But Violet turned from the cosy, easy life of her family to the turbulent militancy of the women's movement for franchise reform – the Women's Social and Political Union, inspired by the Pankhursts. She was an activist with good connections; she was clearly an inspired and busy organiser, first at York and then at Doncaster, where she rented 16, Osborne Road.

Violet moved in there just after the 'Cat and Mouse Act' of 1913 – properly known as Prisoner's Temporary Discharge for Ill Health Act; this followed the furore over forcible feeding as women in prison attempted the strategy of hunger strikes to make their cause known and publicised. It definitely worked, and although the idea was to release women when matters were so grave that they might die in gaol, the effect was to make the militants carry on working, but under an alias.

The whole movement was prominent and there were open fights and disturbances wherever women tried to talk on votes and rights before an assembled crowd. Louts would stone them and heckle them wherever they gathered. The experience of prison also played a part in increasing the sense of militant action in the Suffragette ranks. In prison, they had been very roughly treated; one women, Fanny Halliwell, wrote: 'We had absolutely refused to take food all this time and the doctor was sent for … While waiting for him I amused myself by scratching 'Votes for Women' all over the walls, with the buckle of my belt …' All this lay behind the attitudes of the Doncaster militants.

After the attempt to burn down Westfield House, Harry Johnson was known and the police were looking for him. His possessions were searched and Suffragette literature was found. Harry was soon in a cell, and another accomplice in the attempted arson, Augusta Winship, was identified by Mary Beecroft. He and Violet were to appear at the Doncaster Police Court on 9 June, but there was to be a shock for everyone on that occasion. The place was full and there were eight magistrates on the bench, but there was also someone else. As the Town Clerk began the proceedings the defence sensibly played up the nature of the one witness – Mary Beecroft. They stressed her advanced age and the fact that she wore glasses, and that it had been a dark night. Was she a reliable witness? Apparently she was; but there was a sensation to come when a young woman with long hair took centre stage.

This was a girl said to be 'May Dennis'. In the witness box, she stated outright that she had been the one Beecroft had seen. She had no defence, but stunningly admitted guilt, saying boldly that she entered the property in question to burn it down. Obviously there were gasps of amazement; after all, there had been an old lady asleep upstairs in the place they were to have destroyed. There was a suspicion that this woman was 'Lilian Lenton' – the law was becoming accustomed to identity problems in these suspects by now. She would not give a straight answer to questions about who she was, though, and also gave no more details about the events of the night, or about who she was with when carrying the materials to start a fire.

'May Dennis' was arrested for other crimes, and Harry Johnson was sent to Leeds Assizes (where he was given bail); Winship was released. 'May' was remanded, and there was a lot of rowdy support for her. She had been with Violet at the Osborne Road centre, a hub of militant action. It was asserted in all kinds of places that May was Lilian Lenton, who was notorious, mainly because of her involvement in a fire at Kew Gardens. We have some idea of the extent of the militancy when we note what Sylvia Pankhurst wrote in her memoir: 'Bombs were placed near the Bank of England, at Wheatley Hall, Doncaster, at Oxted Station and on the steps of a Dublin insurance office...'

Lilian had been released under the Cat and Mouse Act and then disappeared from police supervision, but now she had resurfaced. There was a Scotland Yard detective in Doncaster waiting for her; Harry stood with her in Doncaster again, and their offence was serious. Lilian did not plead and followed King Charles II in refusing to acknowledge the status and authority of the court. Then, at Leeds Assizes, Harry was bailed, and Lilian's name hit the national papers: *The Times* described her as 'A fluent prisoner' and went on to say, 'As soon as she appeared in the dock she turned to the jury and announced her intention of not letting the case go on ... As the proceedings started the prisoner began a speech, which lasted until she was finally taken below. After the conclusion of the evidence the judge asked the prisoner, who was now almost breathless, if she had anything further to say to the jury. The irony of the words convulsed the court ...'

In other words, Lilian was causing problems – exactly what she wanted to do. She needed the cause of female suffrage to be in the papers, of course, and she succeeded. She was given a twelve-month sentence but said she would not serve it. The whole place became very noisy and some women were ejected. Lilian was just twenty-two, and Harry Johnson only sixteen. Mr Commissioner Harrison, the judge, had a day he would never forget. Johnson was later sentenced to a year's hard labour in Wakefield prison. The drama of the whole business is further enhanced when we learn, from Jill Liddington, who has researched the case, that there were spy cameras in the prison, and indeed we have a photograph of Lilian, taken in Armley Gaol in June of that year.

Lilian's dramatic story at this time continued with her release from Armley after a hunger strike. In a story in some ways better than crime fiction, she swapped places with an errand boy who came to her address in Leeds, owned by Frank Rutter, a sympathiser with the cause. Disguised as the errand boy, Lilian took off for Harrogate and then later to Scarborough.

Lenton was born in Leicester and trained as a dancer, but she was spurred into Suffragette action by a statement in 1911 by the Prime Minister, Asquith, that more men were going to get the vote, and that votes for women was shelved. She later said, 'I made up my mind that night that as soon as I was twenty-one and my own boss, I would go through these dancing examinations and then volunteer ...' She concentrated on smashing windows and starting fires in empty buildings. But it was one thing to burn down a refreshment pavilion at Kew, and quite another to try to burn down a Doncaster home, ignorant of the fact that an old woman was asleep inside.

But in spite of the arguments and promptings of decency and common sense, it has to be said that Lilian Lenton, alias May Dennis, was a 'fire-starter' in a metaphorical sense as well: Lilian, the daughter of a humble carpenter, became one of the most vociferous and dedicated campaigners that the Pankhursts and others could ever have hoped for. In the context of the Doncaster regime, it is clear that Violet Key Jones was the leader and the planner, and that devotees like Harry Johnson and Lilian Lenton were the activists, the risk-takers. Lilian Lenton was a minor celebrity, her suffering perhaps creating a turning point in the Suffrage movement, because she was dangerously ill after being force-fed, and the Home Secretary at the time, Reginald McKenna, was questioned in the House over the affair. Lilian had become seriously ill in prison after that brutal treatment, contracting septic pneumonia. A surgeon called Victor Horsley wrote to *The Times* to make the point that 'The Home Secretary's attempted denial that Miss Lenton was nearly killed by the force feeding is worthless.'

For that one session in the dock at Doncaster Police Court, the town had its slice of notoriety in the history of votes for women. In the reports at the time, it is clear that there was something extraordinary and charismatic about Lilian Lenton, and her story reads like an adventure novel.

CHAPTER 17

The Goldthorpe Riots
1917

In the general melee two miners named John Burley and John Eades were shot, suffering grave injuries ...

On 7 May 1915, the *Lusitania* was torpedoed by German U-boats off the coast of Ireland. It was a celebrated ship: being launched in 1906, it was the first four-propeller-driven liner, and it was also the largest ship on the seas, weighing in at 40,000 tons. Its loss was a profound shock, and the casualties were very high: 1,195 people drowned. There was a statement by the Germans to justify this, saying that the vessel was potentially something that could be converted into a battleship. It was a signal for anti-German mayhem and disorder across the land, and the Doncaster area had its share of trouble.

There had been immigration into South Yorkshire by German people for a long time: throughout the nineteenth century families settled around the area, bringing businesses such as steel merchants, engineers, cutlery makers, engravers and dentists. After political persecution, notably in 1848 and 1866, the numbers increased. Bradford had always had its German population and its own 'little Germany'. The German contribution to the British economy had been considerable, but then in 1914 we were at war with Germany. When war broke out, there were around 53,000 Germans living in Britain; by the end of the war there were just 22,000. Tens of thousands had been placed in internment camps.

In an order of Council of August 1914, it was decreed that 'aliens' would have to be registered at their nearest police station and they would have to have a permit to move beyond a certain distance from home; there was spy mania across the land, and much popular suspicion of any German names in business.

HINTS FOR THE MAN ON THE BEAT

Get to know all you can respecting your beat—persons, houses, streets, business property.

Obtain a knowledge of all reputed thieves, idle and disorderly persons, and watch closely all persons having no visible means of subsistence.

Always carry your staff and whistle, but be discreet in the use of them.

Do not gossip—but always strive to obtain useful information; it may be very useful to you some day.

Do not loiter or enter any house except in the execution of your duty.

Investigate offences or complaints at once—do not leave them for others to do.

Carefully examine all lock-up property during the time that it is unoccupied. Note especially all doors, windows, fanlights, etc.

Pay strict attention to houses temporarily unoccupied, noting carefully the paths and entrances thereto.

Study the Police Reports, Gazettes, Routes etc.—remember a person wanted in a distant town to-day may be here to-morrow and pass on your beat.

Watch the main road for motor cars reported stolen, etc.

Special Constabulary extracts, 1930. Author's collection

The popular press did not help in clearing any prejudice and irrationality out of the way. Publications such as *John Bull* explained that Germans in Britain were the 'hidden hand' of Kaiser Bill's Reich, and that there was a cunning plan to colonise Britain, starting with these 'aliens'. There was even a suggestion that Germans in Britain should wear a badge or button to show that they were really one of the English citizens of the place, and not aliens.

In April, the nurse, Edith Cavell, had been shot by the Germans, and on 22 April in the trenches, there had been the world's first gas attack in a war. This was followed by an official report on 'Alleged German Atrocities.' This report, priced at only one penny, was 360 pages of myths and provocative statements about Germans doing unspeakable things to women and children. With hindsight, we can see just what an impact this would have had on popular opinion.

Then, the *Lusitania* went down. One report stated that this was 'The most hideous of the many barbarous acts for which the Germans are responsible…' There were savage anti-German riots in Liverpool and special constables were called out in force, operating in makeshift armoured cars. The East End of London was then affected – the very area where one of the most famous of all Germans had lived just a few decades

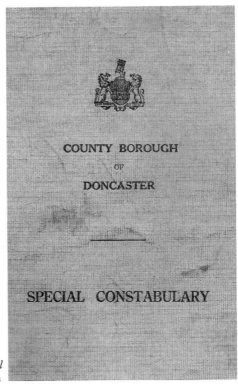

The Handbook of the Special Constabulary. Author's collection

All-British Pianos!!!

SMITH, SONS & CO., 102 & 104, Pinstone St., Sheffield, have sold BRITISH PIANOS exclusively for many years.

What lady or gentleman would ask now for a German-made Piano in preference to one constructed in Great Britain? It would be monstrous!

It would be robbing their own countrymen and putting bread into the mouths of their enemies.

And really and truly for no conceivable cause. Every bit as good a Piano can be made in Great Britain as ever came out of Germany.

Pianos by Hopkinson, Cramer, Collard, &c., &c.

PIANOS from 8/- monthly till paid for.

ORGANS from 5/- monthly till paid for.

PLAYER-PIANOS from 25/- monthly.

DELIVERED FREE.

10 Free Lessons.   Old Instruments taken in exchange.

SMITH, SONS & CO.,
102 & 104, Pinstone St., Sheffield.

'*Buy British Pianos*', *from the* Sheffield & Rotherham Independent, *1914.*
Sheffield & Rotherham Independent

before: Karl Marx. It was clear to the authorities that this violence would spread like a forest fire. It did, and a Mexborough pork butcher called George Schonhut saw his premises utterly destroyed by a crazed mob. Schonhut was a local councillor – far from being any kind of alien. But he had a German name, and that was enough to condemn him. Schonhut was then interned and there was no stated limit on that imprisonment. Then, his cousin Frederick, a Yorkshireman who had been born in Goole, found his business at Goldthorpe was attacked.

Schonhut lost his seat on the Mexborough Borough Council; he was clearly being victimised in all kinds of ways, as he was also summoned for not registering as an alien. He was fined £5 for that omission. The world had gone 'alien mad' – there were even newspaper adverts for 'All-British

Pianos'. The appeal to the public was in these words: 'What lady or gentleman would ask now for a German-made piano in preference to one constructed in Great Britain? It would be monstrous!' Schonhut, ironically, had served Britain in the 1890s, fighting in the Queen's Own Yorkshire Dragoons.

All this was happening in a culture and nation which had a German sovereign and where German arts and music had permeated British sensibilities for centuries, from the advent of Handel in the early eighteenth century to the impact of Brahms at the end of the nineteenth century.

When the Goldthorpe riots started, aimed at Schonhut mainly, there was the usual wild talk – the poor man was supposed to have 'rejoiced' over the *Lusitania* sinking and then it was said that he was violent at home, and 'ill-using his wife'. Any accusation at all could be voiced and the crowd would agree. The spy mania that was turning the people paranoid had it that Schonhut was sending secret messages to Germany, wrapped in packages of his ham.

But then, on Wednesday 12 May, matters were completely out of hand; a man called John Bakewell, who had a business called the London Tea and Drapery Store, was attacked by a huge mob. Amazingly, word was spread around that the man had said he would like to 'wash his hands in English blood'. Bakewell and his two sons, with a friend, were so terrified that they picked up guns to defend themselves. What happened was reported by *The Times*:

> *Serious disturbances in the mining village of Goldthorpe had a sequel yesterday when four men were charged with shooting with intent to cause grievous Bodily harm ... On Tuesday night there were riotous demonstrations against a local butcher of German origin ... On Wednesday the crowd further vented their ill-feeling against another tradesman who is not German, a general dealer named John Bakewell. Extra police were drafted in ... but the mob gained the upper hand and made a furious attack on Bakewell's premises ...*

There was all hell let loose as Bakewell and the three others opened fire on the crowd. Papers later reported that police charged the crowd and had great diffculty 'in keeping the miners in check'. Perhaps, understandably, the Bakewells feared for their lives and took desperate measures. They had taken guns and revolvers and opened fire at random on the threatening crowd. In the general melee two miners named John Burley and John Eades were shot, suffering grave injuries. A grocer's assistant called Thomas Mennell had joined the Bakewells in the shooting. They all appeared before the Doncaster magistrates and were given bail for a week.

Their victims had been seriously injured: Eades had undergone an operation and was recovering and doctors thought he would emerge without serious injury, but Burley was dangerously ill. In terms of the crimes committed by the rioters (because obviously there was looting and criminal damage), at the Doncaster Police Court there were charges against forty-six people and thefts included 'one diamond scarf pin, flitches of bacon and ham and a dynamo'. In fact not only was the shop wrecked, but £3,000 worth of goods were looted according to some reports. The police had been viciously attacked that night as well. A police sergeant who gave evidence later said that the crowd were 'quite mad'.

Eventually, it was decided that charges would not be pressed; the Public Prosecutor and police decided that Bakewell and family had acted in defence of themselves and their property. There was a common feeling that the men in the dock had justification in defending themselves. On the other hand, when some of the looters and rioters were at trial at the Assizes, Bakewell stood as a witness. Several men were given sentences ranging from one to fifteen months of hard labour. As Ernest Pettifer wrote later, in 1939, 'When I remember this crude and senseless outbreak and remember too that there were scenes not greatly dissimilar as recently as 1926, not only in Goldthorpe but in many parts of the Doncaster division, I feel that none of us can afford to be too self-satisfied or complacent as to the alleged improvement in human character.'

CHAPTER 18

The Saga of Sagar
1910–1919

Her story was most unsatisfactory and she was brought before the Justices, on a charge of firing the barn ...

rime historians owe a great deal to professionals in the everyday ranks of the criminal justice system of the past, and this is not often credited. There are dozens of personnel, mentioned in the annual *Law List* who are unsung heroes, playing an important part in the administration of the criminal law in the magistrates' courts and police courts, and most of the time, their lives go unrecorded except for brief mentions in official records. But in Doncaster we have an exception. This was Ernest W Pettifer, who was justices clerk in Doncaster in the first decades of the twentieth century, and he wrote two books of memoirs from his home in Bessacarr. His book, *The Court is Sitting,* provides a rare insight into all manner of criminal cases from the Edwardian years to the late 1930s, and was reprinted twice.

Mr Pettifer gave his main reason for writing the stories linked to Doncaster, and that was that he might be able to 'present to a somewhat critical public some aspects of the task undertaken by the men and women called to act as Justices of the Peace which might mollify their critics ...' In fact, what Mr Pettifer did achieve was a wonderfully anecdotal and dramatic account of several criminals from around Doncaster, but for this story I am recounting the sad tale of one of the clerk's most emotionally charged cases – that of a woman called Alice Sagar, who was a local legend with the police and court officials (to say nothing of press and public) in the years between 1910 and 1919. Her tale is tragic, illustrating the fate of those lawbreakers in the past who ended their lives in institutions such as Broadmoor when in fact they needed

The West Riding Courthouse. Author's collection

professional help much earlier in their lives, long before such desperate measures were taken.

Alice was born in 1894 and became a domestic servant. But her criminal career began with petty thefts over a full year – 1910 – eventually going from being bound over to her first spell in gaol. She was only sixteen when imprisoned for four months. In that period some effort was being made to separate men from women in prisons. In Lincoln prison, for instance, there were men and women together, and children were born in that place, until 1900.

But that was only the beginning of a busy criminal life for Alice. Mr Pettifer saw her first in 1911 when she had stolen £3 and he reckons that it was a chance for her to have a 'fresh start'. But there was something more serious going on around the area – barns were being burned, and also ricks. A tramp was caught near two of these crime scenes and tried at Leeds Assizes, but while he was there, another fire occurred at two barns. Alice was in the frame for these. Police went to find her and they found her in bed, but with her boots on and all her clothes, clogged with manure. She was very wet as well. There was no alibi and no excuses; she was charged and tried at the Assizes. The tramp was still under arrest but was then discharged as it became almost certain that Alice had done this very serious crime. A century before this date arson was a hanging offence.

Alice was only seventeen. It seems amazing to think that she was found not guilty, and reading between the lines, it may be that the jury considered that she needed guidance and a firm hand – but within normal life – rather then festering in a prison. That is all the more ridiculous when we learn that a few weeks later she was found loitering with intent to burn premises again. As Mr Pettifer tells her tale, we have to wonder at her luck in escaping a long stretch with hard labour; but after another theft her story takes a dark and desperate turn as her insanity comes through: she attempted suicide. Alice was waiting her court session when police found her hanging by a rope which had been made from strips of her torn-off clothes. She had tried to use the bars in the cell window. They cut her down but later she tried again, and then, in something so indicative of severe mental illness, in a third attempt on her own life she tried to drown herself in a lavatory bowl.

The obvious destination for such a troublesome teenager then was a spell in Borstal. It has to be recalled that until 1961 suicide was a criminal offence, and in the Edwardian period research has shown that there were very high levels of suicide in working-class communities, for all kinds of reasons. Clearly, mental health was a main factor. The police court missionaries, who had done work with young criminals before there was a probation service (in 1907) often wrote about the dearth of support and understanding for potential suicides. They were often aware that such a thing was a criminal offence, but knew the most common causes, of course, because they knew the people well and spent time with them.

In the case of Alice Sagar, she was in a Borstal for three years. Then she was back in a Doncaster court in October 1913. Borstals were new then: they had been made official in 1908 with some statute law; again, in Alice's case, it was an attempt by the Doncaster bench to be lenient. Young people between the ages of sixteen and twenty-one could be sent to a Borstal for from one to three years as an alternative to a stretch of penal servitude. A young prisoner who did well and showed progress towards rehabilitation could be released on licence after just six months for boys and three months for girls. So once again, she was lucky to be out enjoying her freedom. But in 1913 she was in court for stealing valuable jewels and also for setting fire to a dining room while the family of the house were asleep upstairs.

This meant the end of any lenient thinking about her. She was tried at Assizes by the famous Lord Darling, who said, 'You are the terror of the neighbourhood and the least I can do is to send you to penal servitude for five years.'

In 1919, Mr Pettifer was back after some time away, and Alice had done her time. But she was unreformed, and it can be seen now, through modern eyes, that she had a profound mental illness of a sociopathic kind and was dangerous to anyone she met. She was such a threat in Doncaster, being seen hanging around the police station and even outside the home of the Superintendent, that a policeman was vigilant, watching her through the night.

But there was a switch in behaviour from theft and arson to something strange and extreme. She was seen by the River Dearne in 1914 with a baby in a pram, and she threw pram and baby into the water. A man nearby saved the child, and Alice was caught, destined now to have a mental examination – at last. Mr Pettifer explained the result of the legal and medical deliberations:

At the Assizes the judge put her back for a prolonged medical examination, and this time the report showed definite mental disturbance. She was sent to Broadmoor to be detained during His Majesty's Pleasure and, ultimately, died there...

Ernest Pettifer had his own thoughts about why her course of life was so dangerous and so tragic. He wrote: 'The Justices who monopolised the benches in those days were gentlemen of means and position, many of them of ability but, as a body, they were utterly ignorant of the conditions of the lives of the poor...'

Broadmoor, opened in 1863 in Berkshire, was built as an asylum, not a prison. It was in a rural situation, with great terraces and a high elevation; it did not have an extreme and repressive regime, and Alice would have had proper care for the first time in her life. She could engage in various sports and recreations (including croquet) and none of these gave her any opportunity at all to play with matches or to go anywhere near candles and fires.

Ernest Pettifer spent forty-six years of his life in courtrooms, but very few of the cases he knew could have equalled that of Alice Sagar and her life of destruction – of property, of course – but most of all, destruction of herself. In the vocabulary of that time, she would have been classified as a 'criminal lunatic'. Her saga is one that was being repeated countless times in the busy police courts across the land, especially in London, and in that society in which suicide was a crime, it was left to individuals such as the missionary workers and charities to try to prevent the Sagars of the underclass from the sad downward spiral from petty crime into a place where she would be 'at His Majesty's Pleasure' for her whole life.

CHAPTER 19

Lady Mabel's Slander
1920

I dare not walk about Denaby alone...

In March 1920, Lady Mabel Smith gave a lecture on housing at Denaby. In her speech, these sentences were included after she mentioned that the Urban Power Enquiry stated that the Denaby and Cadeby Main Collieries Limited had land on which they intended to build more housing for miners:

It rests with you now to say how these houses will be built. If you are going to see in the 20th century houses, streets, open courts and all the horrors there are here perpetrated again, I dare not walk about Denaby alone... It incredible to me how you have gone on so long in these conditions. The same conditions exist here today as when I first came. It must be difficult and nearly impossible to bring up your children under proper moral conditions...

Was this a 'true and fair' definition of the housing at Denaby as it existed as Lady Mabel spoke these words? That was the question for the court to decide in July of the same year, when the woman stood accused of slander by the colliery company. WJ Waugh and JW Jardine were the lawyers who had to prove that Lady Mabel was defaming the Company. The result of the case, although Lady Mabel technically lost, was to prove to be a profound criticism of the Company at Denaby, and we might ask where the 'foul deed' lay in this case?

What makes this story particularly interesting is that the lady in question was the daughter of the Earl Fitzwilliam, William Wentworth, Viscount Milton. She married a soldier, Lieutenant Colonel William Smith in 1899 and lived at Ecclesfield. She then became known as Lady Mabel Smith.

She made it plain that she became what some called a 'rabid socialist' after seeing the condition of the children who were living on the Wentworth estate. She and her brother Billy, who ran the estate, did not get on, and she used to tell him that he had so much and everyone else had so little.

She was fifty-one when she made this 'offensive' speech, but she was to spend the rest of her life fighting to improve the lot of the children in the pit villages. She became an active member of the administration of the Workers' Education Authority later. In 1920, when she stood in court, she was speaking of a mining community that had been through some of the most terrible human ordeals one can ever imagine: around the Conisbrough area there had been mines since the late fifteenth century, but since the sinking of the first pit shaft at Denaby, coal had dominated the place. That industry was to bring an excessively tough and demanding working life to the men and squalor for their families. A shaft at nearby Cadeby followed by 1893, and by the time she made that famous speech, there were around 5,000 men working at the two collieries.

The issue in this case is the quality of the housing and amenities built for the mining community and the related topics such as public health and sanitation; there was certainly no shortage of stone or brick in the area: limestone had been quarried there for centuries and there were at least three quarries near Conisbrough. There were also brickyards, one near the castle, but that had closed by the mid-nineteenth century; there was a second yard called Ashfield, which was used until 1960. The jury were taken to see the area in question and Mr Waugh explained the situation in defence of the Company, saying that the firm owned 1,709 houses, and that these were let to the miners.

Lady Mabel and others had expected considerable improvements in miners' housing and public health measures; in 1911 a special conference took place in Doncaster on housing and town planning, and there were representatives of Cadeby and Denaby there. This followed the 1909 Housing and Town Planning Act which was evidence that, at higher levels, politicians and social scientists were concerned about the link between poor housing and epidemics of diseases. The feeling in Doncaster was that something could be done to avoid overcrowding and poor sanitation in pit villages. After all, the industry had a long history of 'jerry-built' housing, attacked so powerfully by DH Lawrence in his essay, *Nottingham and the Mining Country,* in which he is thinking of the unplanned communities and the tendency to build temporary housing. But in the case of the Woodlands Estate, linked to Brodsworth, built in 1907–08, there was evidence that positive change could be achieved. Woodlands had houses with a strip of garden and had water and gas supplies.

One of the main criticisms Lady Mabel had in mind was the midden feature: the outside, shared toilets with night soil collected weekly and shovelled into carts. The present writer, living near Middleton colliery at Leeds, has lived in a village with middens (in the 1950s), and the method was widespread until that decade in many places. My mother and aunts all suffered from illnesses in the 1930s which could be attributed to poor sanitation. In the pit villages close to the shafts the situation was much more extreme.

At the trial in Leeds, Dr Arthur Dunne, Medical Officer of Health for Doncaster Rural District Council, said that the conditions at Denaby were 'most unsatisfactory... the outbreak of enteric fever in Denaby in 1911 was largely due to infection and propagation from the privy middens'. Lady Mabel told the court that she had seen, in day time, the contents of the privy middens emptied into carts, and in her lectures, when she used the word 'horrors' she was demonstrating that the colliery company should not possess the houses of its workers, and therefore have such power to abuse.

Did Lady Mabel have a point? Of course: the Doncaster Regional Planning Scheme, reported on by Abercrombie and Johnson in 1922, stressed that the aims of the 1911 Act, to rationalise housing and planning to incorporate public health issues more intelligently, had not been followed by the Company. In reply at the trial, though, the Company's lawyers said quite the opposite: Harry Warton Smethurst, the Company's architect, said vaguely that 'each batch of houses, with sanitation in mind, was an improvement on the last one'. But that carried little weight beside the point made by

Dr McArthur, who said that with reference to the child mortality – largely from enteritis and diarrhoea – 'the proportion of Denaby to the rest of the district was a high one'.

Naturally, those present in court would have also been aware of the mass evictions at Denaby in 1903. Then, 200 policemen had evicted thousands of people from the village. Almost 300 of those evicted had no home to go to, and marquees were used by church and charities. The Reverend Jesse Wilson, the son of a miner, wrote an account of the events, and perhaps the most poignant scene was this: 'A few feet from the stove were a man and boy lying on a mattress with a thin covering over them. The boy was lying with his face to the man's back... and yet he shivered with cold. His teeth rattled in his mouth...'

Sometimes, the 'foul deeds' were done by those supposedly on the right side of the law. Lady Mabel had a point, and the derisory sum awarded in damages to the Denaby company was the judge's method of telling them that they were morally the losers, if not legally so. The problems went on for miners' housing: even in 1947, the National Union of Miners' *Bulletin*, had a report which reads: 'Asked on March 27th to say what steps are being taken to provide additional housing in mining areas, Secretary to the Minister of Health said that a substantial house-building programme is already in operation... a number of these have been selected by the Coal Board as areas of special need...' In other words, although there had been positive changes (and of course a world war had been fought), the 'special need' was still one of sanitation and housing planning in many areas. At least the 'tintown' villages of the late Victorian years had gone – in which miners' houses were built like temporary blockhouses, the equivalent in today's words of a 'cardboard city'.

In legal terms, a slander 'is not actionable without proof of special damage'. In terms of this case, we are talking about reputation – in slander at that time, the corporal equivalent of a slander which had 'moral opprobrium' cast on a person. In other words, what the Company thought it had to lose, it never actually did have, and its receipt of £5 confirmed that fact. As for Lady Mabel, she had committed a tort, not a crime – a tort being 'a civil wrong for which the victim is entitled to redress'. There was no way that £5 was going to buy a good reputation.

CHAPTER 20

A Dangerous Quack
1924

There is no cure where there is no pain, said Williams.

The historian Owen Davies has explored the byways of popular medicine and folklore in Yorkshire in his book, *Murder, Magic and Madness*, and in that he explains the incredible power of amateur 'wise men' and herbalists in social history: he gives one example of a character in this category from the early nineteenth century: '...the most well-known magical practitioner in Leeds was a wise man named Rough Robin. For much of his career he could be found on a wild spot on Rombalds Moor...People travelled from across the Pennines to consult him...' Even much more recently, in the West Riding and elsewhere, amateur 'medical people' would be consulted to save doctors' bills. But what happened in Doncaster in 1924 beats all of this for sheer crazed danger and pain inflicted on credulous victims. The end of the story is quite tragic and sad, but in the telling, it is shocking.

David Williams was at one time a miner and a farmer, but in his fifties he began to persuade himself that he had special cures for diseases which had beaten the proper medical men. In July 1923, he was in touch with Alice Roe, who was allegedly suffering from cancer. The horrific tale of what he did to his patient was recounted by her daughter, in court before the Doncaster magistrates in January 1924. Valentine Roe, the daughter, said that Williams had told her mother that her illness was cancer and that he had a treatment for it. He looked at the skin and said, 'I have cured many a yellower one than this. I shall have you downstairs and cured in six weeks.'

His treatment involved some toast, on which he poured a mysterious liquid; he explained this substance as being 'brandy but with some special drops'. He applied that and then followed it with some black salve, and then really busied himself with a rare brew of something potent, a combination of a blue-green sugar and some cream, followed by a green ointment that was extremely painful. In fact, as the daughter testified, the poor woman screamed in pain as 'the green ointment caused holes to appear in the affected part'. There was a response to this suffering: this was to state the old maxim: 'There is no cure where there is not pain', said Williams, and the agony went on. In fact, the prosecutor on behalf of the Director of Public Prosecutions, RP Pashley, made the point that the old lady had died earlier than she would have done had she not had this crazy and pointless treatment.

Williams faced a charge of grievous bodily harm, but it was worse – he had taken money from the family as well. Williams was charged with obtaining money by false pretences to the value of £11. After some deliberation, it was suggested that, if Williams' actions were directly contributory to the old lady's death, then there might be a manslaughter charge. But of course, this client was not the first person to be treated by Williams and witnesses were called by the defence. A Mrs Hutchinson said that he had treated her son, who had been considered to be incurable by the doctors, and that she had no regrets in calling out the amateur medical man. It becomes clear reading the report from the Doncaster court that Williams had been working on the desperate and the needy, and those in despair or who might be impoverished. One such was a Mrs Parker, who stated that Williams had treated her and he had given her relief from pain for three weeks, before her sufferings resumed. She wrote a letter which was read out in court, and this read, 'I am a different woman after Williams' treatment. I do not suffer from those nasty pains now. He has done me a world of good. I feel better and brighter.'

But after that, enter the real professionals: first there was Dr EJ Chambers, who had also treated Mrs Parker, and he testified that the amateur therapy did no harm, but also did no good. 'The disease followed its natural course throughout', was his verdict. Mr Pashley questioned the doctor who had treated Mrs Roe, Dr Joseph Walker of Bentley, who pointed out that a caustic substance had been put on the affected area, and this was the heart of the exchange:

> *Mr Pashley: Would she not have lived longer had not Williams treated her?*

> *Dr Walker: She probably would have lived some little time longer.*

> *Mr Pashley: How much longer?*

> *Dr Walker: Perhaps a week or two. Williams' treatment has accelerated the process of exhaustion ...*

Mrs Roe's husband, Frederick, explained about the approach by Williams and about the money he had parted with. The ex-miner had said he could cure his wife, and that £3 per week of treatment was the charge.

There was further evidence of other unfortunates who had crossed Williams' dangerous path. James Woodward was another person considered to be incurable and who was sent home from hospital in Leeds; Williams said he could burn out the roots of the cancer, and applied a lotion. All that happened was that the lotion burned the skin severely. Even worse than this was the torture the victimised Woodward endured when Friar's Balsam was applied to his tongue. The result was a burned tongue and mouth and an inability even to swallow. Again, expert medical evidence confirmed that this would have no effect at all on a cancerous growth.

David Williams' next destination was Leeds Assizes, where he stood before Mr Commissioner Radcliffe. This time Sir HS Cautley was speaking for the prosecution. What happened then was an issue of mental health. Williams had been with a doctor while on remand and there were suspicions that he had serious problems. Cautley reminded the court that the man had used horse liniments with sulphate of copper in his 'cures' and the result had been 'intense pain and suffering' for his supposed patients. The point at debate then was whether or not Williams was fit to stand trial.

The decision was that he was not fit. The Armley Gaol medical officer, Dr Worsley, said he had been studying Williams for three months and had had conversations with him which came to the root of the man's mind: Williams had said that he had a cure for cancer, against all medical knowledge, and that he had been offered £100,000 for this 'miracle cure'. He told the doctor that he had refused to do this and said, 'I expect the Government to pay me even more.' It was looking quite clear that he was deranged: he had told the doctor that he intended to move on from cancer to cure consumption 'and a number of other diseases'.

What then transpired was surely the deciding factor in sealing his fate: he said that he was descended from King George III, that he was a prince who owned 'two-thirds of Wales', and that he was entitled 'to millions of money...which the Government will not let me have'. Williams had written letters to the doctor, stating that he had a vision of God in his cell.

The verdict from the doctor was that Williams was delusional and insane. There was no instruction possible for his counsel and he would have had no understanding of trial proceedings. Williams was destined for an asylum 'at His Majesty's Pleasure'. There may have been complications in homicide cases when it came to insanity defences. But in this case, the prison doctor had no doubt as to the genuine nature of the insanity, despite the fact that some might have said it was a pretence, to avoid a long stretch of penal servitude. That hardly holds water, when we consider the consequences of a spell in an asylum.

CHAPTER 21

Drama in Court
1925

Peeping Toms may deserve an ignominious punishment, but hardly death …

Sometimes in a court of law, the facts are so obscure, and the moral opinions of the jury are so apparent that a skilful barrister will see the way to the light of freedom from the dark cell in which the accused sits. This case is in that category, and it illustrates the nature of that flimsy and malleable line between self-defence and murder.

On 16 December 1924, at the Doncaster cricket field, miner James Doyle, just twenty-three years old, was enjoying a cuddle with his fiancée, Doris Wilford. It was a familiar occurrence of course at that time and surely at all times: two young people wanting some time alone away from the parents and the other elements in life that detract from their time for intimacy. They were engaged to be married – an important factor in the case. But they were certainly not alone.

Two young men called Albert Needham and Wilfred Thrussle, mine surface workers, were in the habit of hanging around the area, spying on courting couples; they were in the habit of hiding behind a wall that skirted the Doncaster cricket ground, and they went to their sneaky business well prepared. They had limelight over them, in the form of a flash-lamp, and Needham even had a rubber knee-cap tied around his leg so that he could noiselessly creep up close and watch the couples from a very close position. But on this night, the two peeping Toms were seen. Doyle walked up to them, seeing the two shapes by the wall, and said, 'What is the game?' He took out a knife and slashed at Needham.

Sir Edward Marshall Hall. Author's collection

The wound was serious – Needham staggered away calling out, 'My God Wilf! He's done it!' The man fell, Wilfred looked down and saw that his friend was dead.

At the Leeds Assizes it was to be a fascinating case, and the great barrister Marshall Hall was to prove something of a hero, being at his very best and most charismatic. Doyle had been carrying a knife and a man had died. As Edward Marjoribanks said in his biography of Hall: 'The question for the jury was, how did this terrible result occur? Allowing for all the outraged anger of a lover pestered by such vile people, the mere curiosity and laughter of peeping Toms armed with a flash-lamp does not justify murder.'

There were muddy footmarks found after the confrontation, on Doyle's waistcoat. So there was a reason for considering self-defence. The motive was not difficult to find, and Mr Justice Branson was told by the judge, Sir Herbert Nield, that the prisoner had taken it upon himself to correct a practice everyone would condemn. But as one writer at the time commented: 'Peeping Toms may deserve an ignominious punishment but hardly death.'

One obvious point made against Doyle was the reasoning that he had suffered at the hands of such people before and went there with the intention of hitting back, teaching them a lesson. But Justice Nield went on to dismiss this with: 'It seems a very far-drawn theory that a lad such embark upon a campaign against such people and should do it in the company of his affianced.' It also became clear that the two men, from South Kirkby, had been busy in this revolting nocturnal hobby for some considerable time. But then it emerged that Wilfred had been the one who had attacked Doyle and this interchange followed with Marshall Hall and the young man in question:

> *'Do you mean to tell the jury,' asked Hall, of the surviving peeping Tom, who was the chief witness for the Crown. 'You were sufficiently expert a kicker to kick this man so high, when he was standing up?' In his evidence, in chief this youth had said, with unashamed frankness, "The latter part of each evening we generally spent in the cricket field, spying on couples."*

Hall asked him if they did it simply for a hobby, for amusement? He stretched out the repulsive nature of the two peeping Toms that there was a sway of feeling against them. The two men loitering were physically bigger than Doyle and Hall made much of that, and argued that, in his anger, Doyle took a knife in order to defend himself. After all, he had had the courage to go and confront two strangers in the dark, alone.

Speaking for Doyle was, first, his auburn-haired fiancée Doris, and then his father, who said, 'A father could not have a better lad.'

Was it going to be a murder charge – or manslaughter? At the coroner's hearing, before coming to Leeds, the charge had been manslaughter. On that occasion Chief Constable Adams of Doncaster had said that Doyle had struggled with two men and in the course of this he 'drew a knife to frighten them'. But at Assizes, Justice Nield was pushing for murder.

The jury retired for an hour and a half, after being told by Hall that, according to the statements made to police and magistrates, Doyle had acted in self-defence. He added: 'He acted in self-defence against two members of a dirty gang who went spying on courting couples. A more incredible, impossible story than that told by Thrussle...was never put before a jury.' Thrussle had painted a picture of a maniac with a knife, enraged at being watched. In contrast, Nield said that the abominable conduct that seemed to be rife in the neighbourhood of the cricket field could not be excused, but he doubted that there was sufficient provocation to make a man 'lose control of himself'.

Was it to be murder or manslaughter? Was there enough evidence to suggest that young Doyle had pulled and used his knife after extreme provocation? Looking at the case now, that situation appears to be very unlikely. But Sir Edward Marshall Hall was impressive and persuasive: Doyle was acquitted. He was never called to give evidence himself in the course of the trial. What became known as 'The Peeping Tom Case' went down in the annals of Doncaster crime as one of the most controversial. Marshall Hall had enhanced his already formidable reputation and James Doyle went home to marry his Doris, rather than take a trip to the condemned cell.

CHAPTER 22

'I Have Killed a Woman'
1927

I have left her by the sink and the razor is by her head.

I n Westgate, Hemsworth, Robert Moore and his family must have appeared to be living a normal, ordinary life to anyone who might stop to consider them. Robert was married to Isabella, and they had two small children. The only odd thing was that, to echo a statement from a much more famous but troubled relationship, 'There were three of us in this marriage.' The third party was a certain Arthur Harnett: he was just twenty-eight and Isabella Moore was thirty-three and they were good friends. But the apparent normality of the classic *ménage à trois* applies here. There were emotions running deep and cutting hard in this case, and to this day, the reasons for what happened are very obscure.

Matters were very strained though, and Robert was worried and suspicious; he had it out with his wife and demanded the truth about her 'friend' and Isabella swore that there was nothing else but friendship to her time spent with Harnett; Robert had banned Harnett from calling again, but he relented and allowed him to return after these assurances. But then, one day in June 1927, everything in Robert Moore's life was to be shattered, and his first inkling of trouble was when he came home from work and saw a constable, Henry Sagar, at his doorstep. Robert knew that his wife had said she was going out – to the YMCA in fact – but that hardly gave him cause for concern when he saw the police at his home.

But at that point the officer had not entered the house: he had simply come after a call, and was told to find out what was the problem. He and Moore then went inside and when they reached the little scullery, there was Isabella, lying dead. But there was to be no murder hunt, because Arthur Harnett had paid a visit to the Blue Bell Hotel, given his watch and military medals to a friend, and made it clear that he would not need them any more. He said, 'I have killed a woman.' He added some more words, plain and direct: 'I have left her by the sink and the razor is by her head.' It must have seemed to the drinking mate that the man was in some kind of trance. But Harnett had gone from wanting some cash for the watch to simply giving it away – markedly strange behaviour by any standards.

Then Harnett simply walked to Market Street and there he met Sagar, telling him to take him inside because he had, as he said, 'Done something serious.' When questioned, he could give no explanation for the horrible thing he had done, and that was important as matters progressed. Those few spoken words turned out to be a massive understatement. There had been a bloody, savage murder.

In Pontefract, Harnett stood on a murder charge. All Moore could say was that he and Sagar had had to force the house door open when there was no other way in, she having taken the key. Through his ragged emotions, Moore managed to tell the tale of witnessing Harnett's friendship with his wife grow over the last year, but he said that he had only known Harnett (that he was the 'other man') for the last three months and that he had had strong words with him. Harnett pleaded not guilty and reserved his defence.

At Leeds Assizes there was an attempt at a defence of insanity, and it was a genetic factor. On top of that, Moore told the court that Harnett had suffered from malaria, but any influence on him that might have made insanity a possibility was dismissed. There was at that time very little room for manoeuvre in such attempts at establishing a defence of insanity; but after the trial the case went to appeal. GW Wrangham spoke for Harnett and the claim was for a misdirection to the jury by the judge at the first trial. Wrangham claimed that the accused had often been seen leaving the Moores' house at the time of the murder, so that would have intensified the feeling about his guilt in the mind of the jury of course. The claim was that the evidence of the identity of the man seen leaving the house on those several occasions was not conclusively a naming of Harnett. None of this achieved anything. Mr Justice Swift, presiding, said, 'The evidence was properly laid before the jury at Leeds, and no exception may be taken to the nature of the initial summing-up.' The appeal was therefore dismissed. Most events at the court of criminal appeal at the time were brief, and there were few acquittals in what reads today as a long succession of household-centred family violence and homicide.

Harnett was destined to be a victim of Thomas Pierrepoint the hangman, at Armley Gaol, on 2 September. This year,1927, had a heavy toll of hangings, and Pierrepoint performed four in England and one in Ireland. Harnett's was just one of dozens of killings in the ten years after the Great War in which razors were used as the murder weapon – and they were mostly domestic murders, husbands killing wives. Many were due to mental illness resulting from neurasthenia or shell shock in the trenches; there was no way that Harnett was in that category, though. His motive remains clouded in mystery as there were no witnesses and he gave no lucid explanation of his barbaric killing.

Insanity in the accused was never in question, but as a coda to this sad tale, we may note that just a few months later, again at Leeds Assizes, there was a case of which there was no doubt at all about an insane state of mind: Harry Troman was found insane and unfit to plead. He had locked himself and his son in a bedroom and then shouted at the police to stay away. When the officers thought Troman was asleep they went in, and the man struck the child on the head with a poker. The lawyers did not have to work hard on that one when the question of a viable defence arose, but he was unable to appear in court anyway. That *was* insanity.

CHAPTER 23

Steve Hangs a 'Local'
1947

A cigarette stump had been forced into her vagina ...

There are crimes of passion and there are absolute crimes of barbarity. This is the story of one of the latter variety, and it happened in a Doncaster house.

Constable Douglas Porter was called to a murder scene on 9 October 1947, in Wainwright Road: Doris Corcoran, who was next-door neighbour to the Parkin family, saw that the door of the house was open and, as she looked, with neighbourly concern, Doris saw the body of Maurice Parkin. Another neighbour, Kathleen Mitchell, had called earlier to walk to work with Joyce Parkin, but there had been no answer.

The body had been in the scullery for at least six hours when PC Porter arrived. There was a shock in store for the policeman, because in the living room there was another body – Maurice's sister Joyce and their mother Alison. It was horrific: the women had their legs spread wide apart, and on closer inspection, it was found that Maurice's trousers were pulled down and there was a bloody mess around his crotch.

When the medical men arrived the full horror was revealed: Maurice Parkin had no genitals and they eventually found them in his mother's mouth. There was a further shock in store, as they studied the body of the mother closely and found that a cigarette stump had been forced into her vagina. The daughter, Joyce, had a cigarette end stuffed down her throat. The three victims had all been strangled, and it was clear that the killer was known to the family as there had been no evidence of anyone forcing their way into the house.

Enquiries led to a driver with the Blue Line Bus Company called George Whelpton. He was thirty-one, and had been seeing Alison Parkin for a short time; he was married, and the

The Town Hall, Leeds (Assizes). Author's collection

affair had been a hard one, highly emotional. The police took Whelpton in for questioning after he arrived at the Company offices to collect his wages. It emerged that he had been for a meal with the Parkins, and after Maurice and his mother had retired to bed, George and Joyce had an argument about money. George told police that he had been attacked by the woman and had then fought back and strangled her. His story was that Maurice had heard the row and come down to confront him; George had a boiling temper by this time, he claimed, and when Maurice came at him, he responded by grabbing him and strangling him also. The mother appeared next and she had the same treatment. The killer said that he could not recall the attack he made on the mother and son. That was his story.

But in court, in Leeds, the actual events of that horrendous day were revealed. Whelpton had called and had sex with the sister, Joyce. Alison found them *in flagrante delicto* and the man went berserk, killing both women. Maurice was then also strangled because he would have made the whole business public of course. It was a vicious triple murder, something that escalated into what appeared like the ravages of a madman when the police and medical experts arrived at the house. In court, the defence of insanity was attempted, clearly with that thought in mind – that the evidence at the crime scene would have initially suggested a crazed, perhaps even motiveless attack.

The jury accepted the story of the sex with Joyce and the 'crime of passion' line of defence was never even attempted. Everything pointed to a desperate and brutal attack by a powerful man. It took a lot of strength to strangle three adults, so the killer was totally determined to stifle (literally) the possibility of his misdeeds becoming known. He thought he could go back to work, live normally again, and be allowed to get on with life. How wrong he was.

Local man Steve Wade ironically owned a bus company in Doncaster, based at Waterdale. Now he found himself lined up to be the hangman who would execute his local victim, Whelpton. Wade was busy in 1947 and early 1948, taking over as principal hangman after being assistant to Albert Pierrepoint, who was away in Germany hanging Nazis when Whelpton walked out onto the scaffold at Armley on 7 January 1948. Wade and his assistant, Harry Kirk, knew the full facts, and it had to be one of the least problematical cases for them. Wade and Kirk had, within the previous year, teamed up to hang four woman-killers, and the businessman from Doncaster with one of the most demanding part-time jobs possible was hardened to the job by the time he dealt with Whelpton.

Wade was a heavy smoker and he liked a drink, but he was a skilled craftsman with the rope and the drop. George Whelpton left this world at the hands of two seasoned professionals who knew how to 'stretch' a man efficiently.

CHAPTER 24

The Mysterious 'Peace' Man
1952

I signed my name on that paper, I have been in the very depths of hell ...

This is a melancholy tale of what can happen when so-called 'people of conscience' and pacifist movements attract people who are not only politicised but unbalanced. Clearly, the anonymous villain of this tale was hardly a typical member of any group.

In the early 1950s there was a strong protest movement against supposed atrocities by American servicemen in Korea. The USA had occupied Korea in September 1945. After that there were alleged offences and brutalities by soldiers, figures quoted being 'hundreds of cases of murder, rape and robbery'.

The 'Peace' Man, headline in the Sunday Dispatch, *1952.* Sunday Dispatch

The Peace Committees across the country were linked with Communists and even the word 'Communist' was, in many quarters, equated with 'traitor'.

That is the background to what is a terrible case of suicide. It began one day in February 1952 when a man called at the home of a miner, Charles Perry, in Askern. Mrs Mary Perry was at home and the man abruptly asked her, 'Do you want peace?' He then thrust a sheet of paper at her and said, that if she did, she should sign the paper. Mary Perry was worried about what she had done and she mentioned it to her husband when he came home. She checked with him whether or not she should have signed it. Charles Perry said that he would not have done so. That seems to have been the source of what became a profound anxiety on Mary's part.

Mr Perry told a reporter from the *Sunday Dispatch*, Anthony Hunter, later that his wife had said nothing in reply. But looking back, there was some concern in her. But what she thought was some kind of terrible crime rankled in her, and Mary Perry, a few weeks later, cleaned the house, then put on her best clothes and sat down to write a letter to her husband. She wrote: 'I want to tell you here and now how much I love you. I am not worthy of you. I signed my name on that paper. I have been in the very depths of hell.' What Mary Perry did next was horrendous to contemplate.

She hanged herself from the lintel of the living room door. It is impossible to imagine what Charles Perry must have felt shiver through his very soul when he came home to that sight. Mary had written that she was 'a traitor to her country' and that appears to have been the central, determining thought behind her suicide.

Charles had the help and solidarity of other miners when it was known that the stranger had come to the house with the petition from the Peace Committee. Several men in the village made it known that they intended to mob any member of the Doncaster Peace Committee who dared to come looking for signatures in the area. Charles Perry then took to the road, hunting for the man. He left his three children with relatives and started his search, but it was a hopeless task. He went to see the police, the coroner and of course, to the Communist

Party locally, and to the secretary of the Peace Committee. The petition had the signature of Arthur Horner, a noted Communist, and other members of the Communist Party, but the Peace Committee secretary assured Charles that the Communists were not behind the petition.

Mary was just thirty-four years old. Her visitor had been a tall, well-spoken man and he had talked of the Korean War, and his talk of the supposed awful atrocities was surely the influential part of his persuasive chat with Mary. In fact, even today, there is still an online petition for that same cause. In 2005, the sixtieth anniversary of the US occupation, the writers of that petition claimed that 'The armistice signed at the end of the Korean War was a temporary ceasefire, not a peace treaty' and that 'The legal mechanism governing US occupation... is an unequal treaty that enables US soldiers to act with impunity against Korean civilians'.

It is not hard to imagine that the stranger in Doncaster spoke in that exact way, probably addressing Mary in the second person: 'You would not want this to carry on would you?' But whatever he said or did, he was never found. Charles Perry had to live with the knowledge that a stranger had come to his house and spoken to his wife in such a way that he drove her to a guilt and remorse she could not tolerate.

Some crimes – 'foul deeds' – are never punished, and some, like this one, do not even have a name, a classification. The man went on to spread his extremism and prejudice, hopefully not with more impressionable people like Mary Perry.

CHAPTER 25

Obscene or Not?
1954

Unless you come to the conclusion that these books are lewd or
filthy they cannot be classed as obscene…

In the 1950s, before the *Lady Chatterley* Trial of
1960, the British legal machine had a problem with
the notion of what was 'obscene' and what was not.
The statistics tell the pathetic story: destruction
orders were granted for 167,293 books and magazines; the
number of convictions for publishing obscene material more
than doubled from 49 to 111. Anything with a sexual content,
even the infamous Kinsey Reports, *Sexual Behaviour in the
Human Male* (1948) and *Sexual Behaviour of the Human
Female* (1953) were likely to attract the law. In fact, it has been
shown by social historians that throughout the nineteenth
century and into the Edwardian years, a modernised version
of a work by the classical Greek philosopher, Aristotle, was the
standard sex manual for young married people, and was often
passed from father to son. In other words, British culture in
the 1950s had a huge problem with sexuality and knowledge.
The great fear was that children and young people, if they
were not taught biology and sex in school would 'learn from
toilet walls' and of course, from supposed 'filthy literature'. I
was at school in the 1950s and I can say that in working-class
Leeds, our biology involved cutting up cows' eyes, not classes
in which we were taught about human sexuality. What was
written on the school toilet walls provided nothing educational
whatsoever. In the early years of there 1950s there were
extreme measures taken, across the land, against anything in
print that might be obscene. The word needs legal explanation
first: 'a publication, the tendency of which is to deprave and
corrupt those whose minds are open to immoral influences and

into whose hands it is likely to fall' (*Osborn's Concise Law Dictionary*). The problem is the slippery nature of the words 'deprave and corrupt' and also the word 'immoral'. All these terms are, of course, very hard to define in universal terms. The real complication here is that those writings which instruct and enlighten may do so by means which some minds may consider to be corrupt, of course, and there is the dilemma.

The basis of much of this thinking lies in the Obscene Publications Act of 1857 which defines as a misdemeanour any so defined publications circulated for sale, exhibition or purposes of gain. The post-war years in Britain saw all kinds of specific legislation to broaden the scope of that Act, such as the Post Office Act of 1953 which made it an offence to send indecent books or prints through the post, punishable on indictment by a maximum of twelve months' imprisonment or on a summary conviction of a fine of £10. Even the artist Donald McGill, of 'naughty seaside post card' fame, was summonsed and fined.

In Doncaster, Edward Elvidge had a shop in St Sepulchre Gate in which he sold a variety of printed matter relating to sex education. His shop was not really a bookshop, in the sense that its window displays and business terms suggested that he was running something described as being 'merchants, manufacturers and importers'. He explained to the Doncaster magistrates on March 20 that 'One of the windows contains tricks, puzzles, and jokes of all kinds, appealing to the young mind.' Mr Elvidge was in court after a quantity of his merchandise, 155 obscene books and 3,688 photographic representations, were seized and destroyed.

Mr Percy defended Elvidge, and the shopkeeper asserted that he would resist an order for all the seized materials. The prosecutor, Mr Barlow, pointed out that the Kinsey reports were 'reputable' but that the point was that 'the books are obscene in the circumstances in which they are sold'. What he meant by that was that Mr Elvidge was actually providing an educational service for the public. Mr Barlow also said, after reading an extract from Kinsey, that there was good ground for thinking that the printed matter sold in the shop would 'deprave and corrupt'.

Elvidge's defence was that he was a wholesaler doing valuable work, for instance, in providing literature for people about to get married. He said that couples called and said, 'We are getting married next month, can you supply us with a little book?' The shopkeeper said that if he thought a person was 'not the right type' he would not sell him anything. His educational crusade was further explained when he told the court: 'Certain books are marked for sale to physicians, teachers, nurses and clergymen. I have sold quite a few of the books to doctors.'

Mr Percy reminded the magistrates of the difficulty of defining what was obscene. He said, 'What an emptying of bookshelves there would be if you decided that all the books before you were obscene. Unless you come to the conclusion that these books are lewd or filthy they cannot be classed as obscene...' What made it complicated was that Elvidge had stocked the *Kinsey Report*, and that had not been classed as obscene elsewhere.

The magistrates found that the Kinsey publication was not obscene, but ordered that all the other books and photographs from Elvidge's shop should be destroyed. Less than a year after this hearing, there was a bill to ban horror comics or 'harmful publications' as they were called; the penalties were extreme, including a fine of £1,000 and four months in prison. The fact about the Doncaster case is that it was not at all related to the general fears about the fantasies of the young linked to the glamour of such things as gun crime. It was merely a provision of an outlet for knowledge of and interest in sex – and at a time when there was still a huge and widespread taboo in most areas of society in the area of open discussion about sex education. It may well be that Mr Elvidge was indeed supplying an educational need in the public, but then unfortunately his only system of vetting who read and who bought his materials was whether they looked suitable for such a purchase. That would not have impressed the bench.

The magistrates simply said, 'destroy these books' and after extracts were read to the court, no doubt causing some uncomfortable shifting on the seats, there was no doubt that this was not, in the terms of 1954, a wholesome trade to have going on in the heart of Doncaster. It was hardly a job for Scotland Yard's Obscene Publications Squad, but it was a warning of what was still to come for DH Lawrence's sexy novel and for Penguin Books who were daring enough to publish. The record shows that *Lady Chatterley's Lover* was, as Mr Elvidge would have agreed, suitable for teachers, doctors and clergymen: in other words, a select readership who, it had been assumed, could not be depraved and corrupted.

CHAPTER 26

Cops and Robbers at Carlton Loop 1955

Norton bravely managed to stagger a mile to the nearest police station.

I t is not exactly in the public mind to think of the railway policeman with the same glamour and sense of drama that the police officer 'on the front line' might have applied to him, or her. But that is a media myth. The reality is that the railway police have always had a particularly tough job. When it is considered just how much distance of line has to be patrolled and just how much vigilance is required in the kind of crime that is often done by night, then the nature of their task becomes more apparent. The Great Train Robbery captured the imagination of writers and film-makers, but that was extraordinary in every sense. In the days of steam, the vulnerability of the carriages was remarkably acute; an organised gang could wreak havoc in a short time and disappear into the night.

The railways in the 1950s were prey to all kinds of desperate gangs of robbers, as indeed shops and factories were: it was a time of armed robbery and villains who would do anything to escape capture. As railway historian JR Whitbread has pointed out, 'The sidings are among the worst places to guard, lonely places in which it is most difficult for a detective to maintain observation and actually to catch a thief in the act.' To combat robberies from carriages in sidings, railway police used dogs, but in the Doncaster area in 1955, even the dogs were no problem to one particular gang.

There had been a series of robberies from the railways around the Doncaster area at this time and, on one raid, the police dog in pursuit of the robbers was knocked out. The situation was extreme, and extreme measures were needed, so

Map showing the railway line south of Doncaster, towards Carlton Loop. Cassini Maps

the police decided to set up a close surveillance on one stretch, and that was at Carlton Loop on the Doncaster to Newark line. It was going to be tough; in recent years two railway policemen had been killed on this kind of active service against men who would stop at nothing to get away with their booty.

RAILWAY POLICEMEN WOUNDED

HEAVY SENTENCES ON THREE MEN

Leonard Mangham, aged 43, miner, of Foundry Lane, Mexborough, at Nottinghamshire Assizes yesterday was sentenced to 14 years' preventive detention for wounding two railway policemen, Ronald Norton and Sidney Metcalfe, with intent to cause grievous bodily harm, and causing grievous bodily harm to a third officer, Derick Cook, with intent to resist arrest. He was sentenced to eight years' preventive detention on a third charge of stealing clothing worth £89, the property of the British Transport Commission, and a fourth of stealing a bicycle, the sentences to run concurrently.

Mangham's son, Arthur Mangham, aged 22, also of Foundry Lane, Mexborough, was sentenced to eight years' imprisonment on the first two charges and five years on the third, to run concurrently. Jack Hirst, aged 44, of Common Lane, Mexborough, was sentenced to eight years' preventive detention on the first two charges and eight years' preventive detention on the third, the sentences to run concurrently.

The three men were convicted last night after a three hours' retirement by the jury, who found them Not Guilty of wounding Norton and Metcalfe with intent to murder, with intent to resist arrest. In the case of Eric Bowen, aged 29, of Fitzwilliam Street, Swinton, Yorkshire, who appeared with the other three, the jury said that they could not

One night, as police watched that stretch of line, a Doncaster-bound goods train came to the Loop and then officers saw that there were torch lights and that items were being thrown from the train. After the train then pulled away, a gang of five men was visible. It was a direct confrontation, police against the gang, and it was no holds barred. The weapons used were anything close to hand, but there was one specific attack that almost killed Constable Norton: this was a rope with a hook, a tool used in the robbery to grab a side of a carriage. The man swinging this rope and hook, Arthur Mangham, went at the officer mercilessly with the thing, and the hook was lodged in the policeman's head. What had accelerated the scrap was that one of the robbers had been brought down and then cried for help. One of the five had run away and was not seen again, so four were standing, at bay, ready for anything, and the use of the hook was no worry to them.

The other constables, Metcalfe and Cook, were also battered about the head and the gang escaped. Norton was severely wounded. But he was not going to just lie there and wait to see who arrived. While Cook was carrying Metcalfe to the crossing-keeper's house so that medical help could be called, Norton bravely managed to stagger a mile to the nearest police station. When he finally walked into the station, the daughter of a sergeant fainted, so horrible was the bloody sight before her. There were several incredibly impressive actions that night, not the least of which was the medical help given to Metcalfe by the keeper, who probably saved the man's life. The officer had been knocked out by a lead-filled stick, a kind of home-made truncheon.

But there was no difficulty in contacting probable suspects. The gang, led by Butch Mangham, was the outfit most likely responsible. He had a record, and his house was under surveillance immediately after this fight. It was noticed that Butch's son Arthur came, and then walked out to bury something. Fingerprints helped to track down another man in the gang, called Jack Hirst. The buried items proved to be the rope and hook and some bolt-croppers. The last robber in the fight, a man called Bowen, was then tracked down. All four were arrested, and of course, there had been injuries so severe to the police officers that the charges were very grave. The arrest was not easy, of course. The son was taken first and, as expected, Leonard 'Butch' put up a fight but was overpowered. Police were taking no chances this time. Of course, it was daylight, so any unspeakably nasty weapons in store for them would have been seen this time, and they were prepared for a determined resistance.

'Butch' was Leonard Mangham, and his son Arthur, and Hirst, were given heavy sentences in gaol. Butch was given fourteen years for grievous bodily harm (on Norton and Metcalfe) and also on Constable Cook. He had also resisted arrest. Jack Hirst was given eight years' detention and Arthur Mangham had eight years to serve. The gang were from

Mexborough: Butch was a miner and as tough as they come. He had clearly been quite able to take on several men, and was ruthless enough to fight with anything to hand and not worry about the consequences. That is why there was a first charge of wounding with intent to murder. The jury took three hours to decide, at Nottingham Assizes, that they were not guilty of that charge. The judge told Butch Mangham, 'You have done this kind of thing too often...and this time you have done it on a grand scale...'

Naturally, there were honours due to the courageous and plucky constables: at first they received letters of commendation, but later they were awarded the Queen's Commendation 'for services when a gang of violent and dangerous criminals attempted to rob a railway goods-van'.

CHAPTER 27

Doncaster's Hangman

*In Balby archives we have pencilled notes on his hangings, and a
card expressing thanks from Winston Churchill.*

Steve Wade comes down to us from one photograph;
our image of him is of a man with a drink and a
cigarette, the face suggesting someone under
pressure, maybe a nervous type. That is not
associated with a hangman, of course. What the image does
convey is that he was maybe ill when the picture was done. He
was not in office long – from 1941 to 1955 – and had to retire
through ill health. He died in 1959, having been assistant to
both Tom and Albert Pierrepoint. Steve handled twenty-nine
hangings as chief executioner, and he had some really difficult
cases.

He once said that he 'carried out more executions than I
could remember' and that suggests a man who was not
necessarily meticulous. He also pointed out that the hanging
was a sideline. Indeed it was, because he was in the transport
business in Doncaster. If a full biography of him was ever
written, the sub-title might read, 'Executioner and bus owner'.
When he wrote to the Home Office to offer his services, he was
at first refused as he was so young, but Wade must have been
determined because he wrote again later and then was
accepted. He was placed on a waiting list and given the usual
course of instruction, before being appointed deputy to
Thomas Pierrepoint.

Wade went to live in Doncaster in 1935 and he established
his coaching business in the Waterdale area. He must have had
a sense of humour (very dark) because, according to Brian
Bailey, Wade tricked Albert Pierrepoint into thinking that both
he and Wade were needed to be at the post-mortem of a young

man from Burma who had murdered his wife, after they had executed the man. The pathologist involved was the famous Keith Simpson. According to Molly Lefebure, who was Simpson's secretary at the time, Pierrepoint walked into the set-up scene and said, 'If you don't mind, I'd like to take a look at my handiwork.' That hardly seems in keeping with the man, and if he did, he would have seen a fracture dislocation between the second and third cervical vertebrae. Bailey makes the point that such a detail signifies the quickest and 'cleanest' death for a victim of the hangman's art.

Wade's first job as assistant was with Tom Pierrepoint at Wandsworth, where they hanged George Armstrong, a man who spied for Germany, starting that work after contacting a German consul in the USA. He was tried at the Old Bailey, then appealed and after that failed, found himself facing the noose.

But before Steve Wade began his main work in Yorkshire, he had a job with Albert hanging another spy that turned out to be a terrible ordeal. Wade took a few notes on jobs, and a typical one is this one on William Cooper at Bedford in 1940. Tom and Albert were the official hangmen, but Wade must have been there to observe and to learn, because he made these notes:

William Henry Cooper at Bedford, aged 24. Height, five feet five and a half inches. Weight 136lbs. Drop 8 feet one inch. Assisted to Scaffold. Hanged 9 a.m. on Nov. 26 1940.

He notes that the personnel present were 'Pierrepoint, Wade and Allen' but that does not tally with the official record.

As time went on he wrote more, as in the case of Mancini for which he stated, 'Three appeals with the House of Lords'. But the ordeal was to come with the execution of the spy Karel Richter. Richter's records have now been released and we know that his mission was to deliver funds and a spare wireless crystal to another spy. He was given a code and money and also a supply of secret ink and was even briefed on what to say if interrogated. Acccording to some opinions, his arrival on espionage work was part of a 'double-cross' system which meant that agents were captured and given an option either to work as double agents or to face the gallows.

Richter was parachuted into Hertfordshire in 1941 and it appears that Churchill wanted him executed, as other agents had landed and not been hanged. That might be arguable, but what happened, according to MI5, is that Richter landed on the 14 May and that war reserve constable Boott at London Colney saw a lorry driver talking to a man who turned out to be the spy. Sergeant Palmer of St Albans was informed and came to assist. Richter was taken to Fleetville Police Station and there he showed a Czech passport. When searched, he had a ration book, a compass, cash and a map of East Anglia.

Richter was seen by a girl, Florrie Cowley (née Chapman), who recalls going to visit her divisional campsite, of the guides, at Colney heath and that she and a friend went into a storage hut. There they saw evidence of very recent occupation. She wrote in a memoir, 'We quickly came out to think the situation over. Being war time there were no vagabonds, tramps etc. around so who could be living there? We then thought a German spy could have dropped...' They were right. Photographs survive of Richter going back to the field with army and police to find his buried equipment. Richter stands in one photograph, pointing, while surrounded by personnel. He was destined to be Pierrepoint and Wade's client on 10 December 1941.

Wade kept notes on what happened that day. It was a horrendous experience for the young hangman, so early in his career. First he wrote, 'Karl Richter, 29 five feet and eleven and a half inches. 172 lbs. Execution: good under the circumstances'. That has to be one of the greatest understatements ever written. Richter was athletic, strong and determined to cause the maximum resistance when the hangmen arrived at the death-cell. Wade wrote:

On entering cell to take prisoner over and pinion him he made a bolt towards the door. I warded him off and he then charged the wall at a terrific force with his head. This made him most violent.

We seized him and strapped his arms at rear ... The belt was faulty, not enough eyelid holes, and he broke away from them. I shouted to Albert 'He is loose' and he was held by warders until we made him secure. He could not take it and charged again for the wall screaming HELP ME.

Things were still very difficult, as the man then had to be manhandled by several warders. Even at the scaffold, Richter fought:

... he then tried to get to the opposite wall over trap. Legs splayed. I drew them together and see Albert going to the lever. I shout wait, strap on legs and down he goes. As rope was fixed around his neck he shook his head and the safety ring, too big, slips ...

Wade's notes have a tone of relief as he writes finally, 'Neck broken immediately'.

At the end of his notes he wrote that he said something to Albert, a comment along the lines of 'I would not miss this for fifty pounds ...'

Richter actually stated under questioning that he had declined to take a part in the 'double cross system'. He had been a marine engineer and had a child in the USA. He was interned and returned to Germany after trying to return to America. In Germany he was recruited by the Abwehr (the German intelligence and counter-intelligence organisation). Nigel West, in his history of MI5, has a coda to add to Steve Wade's terrible memoir:

The grisly scene had a profound effect on all those present, and, indirectly, on some other Abwehr agents. Several months later Pierrepoint and his chief assistant, Steve Wade, carried out an execution at Mountjoy in Dublin. News of Richter's final moments reached Gunther Schutz and his fellow internees ... Irish warders gleefully recounted the details of the struggle on the scaffold, sending Richter's former colleagues into a deep depression.

In Balby archives we have pencilled notes on his hangings and a card expressing thanks from Winston Churchill.

From 1947, Wade did several hangings in Leeds, beginning with Albert Sabin from Morley, who murdered Dr Neil Macleod at Topcliffe Pit Lane in Morley, in 1947. Sabin had been seen running and getting into, the doctor's car in the early afternoon of 21 September 1946. Sabin was just twenty-one, and in his army uniform. At around half past two that same day a shot was heard in the lane.

The doctor was found dead only a short time after his murder, by Harry Philpott, as he was walking near to the Topcliffe pit. The scene was like one of Hitchcock's more macabre episodes, as poor Harry followed a trail of blood, then a knife and finally a gun. Then there was the body of MacLeod in a hollow, having been shot three times as it turned out.

The hunt was on for the doctor's car, a Ford V8. It was not a difficult task in those naïve days when occasional, opportunist criminals (unlike the professionals of course) merely took their victim's property and did not think too much about forward planning. Sabin was found at Pudsey, where his car was parked, and arrested. There was also no question of any mind games or ploys to buy time and cause trouble: Sabin simply confessed to the killing when accosted.

The issue was whether or not this was a murder; but it was ascertained that Sabin took the gun with him when he went to meet the doctor, and that he had at least an intention to rob, and most likely to do grievous bodily harm if resisted. Taking the victim's life was merely one more step away from that, with a related intention of 'malice aforethought'. The only further complication came later when the killer tried to say that the doctor had made sexual advances to him; there were semen stains found on clothing, but they could have occurred just as naturally as part of the shock of death as much as in a sexual encounter, so nothing was conclusive there. Sabin claimed that on the day of the murder, Macleod had said he would give Sabin a lift back to camp, but then had driven to a place where he could make his advances. Naturally, Sabin tried to construct a narrative which culminated in a struggle and consequently that the gun had fired with no intention on Sabin's part to take life. That story did not convince the jury

and Steve Wade, along with Harry Kirk, had a client at Armley
– just twenty-one and a hardened killer – waiting for them in
the death cell in January 1947.

The team of Wade and Kirk were busy in the summer of
that year at Leeds. Wade and Kirk did three hangings by the
end of 1949 and Wade had another assistant for yet another
Leeds execution in that eighteen months. Wade's victims
were from that area of life we might call domestic-tragic.
Their killings were of women, either known to them or
prostitutes. The men waiting for the noose at Armley were
invariably killers driven by sexual passion, or aggression
while drunk, or of course, a combination of all these. Typical
was the case of the sad murder of Edith Simmonite in
Sheffield. Edith spent a night enjoying a few drinks in the
Sun Inn and she had been in company with two men who
lived at a nearby hostel – William Smedley being one of
them. On the night on which someone murdered Edith,
Smedley's bed at West Bar had not been slept in. There were
sound testimonies to that fact later.

So when Edith's body was found, strangled and after
having sex, it was a case of basic police work to find out who
she had been with and where she had spent her time that day.
The task was made even more straightforward by the fact
that she was known to the police as a local prostitute. When
questioned, Smedley clearly relied on the man with him to
back him up in a lie – that the two men had parted from the
woman that night and seen her go into her room. Smedley's
tale was not verified by his companion, and so the option
open to him then was to invent another suspect. He did this
by inventing 'an Irishman' who had ostensibly been in
Edith's company. He even claimed that the mysterious
Irishman had confessed to the murder to him (Smedley).
Smedley had been interviewed twice, and told a plausible
tale, so was released on both occasions.

What was also very disturbing and seedy about this case was
that Edith's body was found by a young boy. Peter Johnson
was out looking for wood in the old buildings in the areas of
the city that had received bomb damage when he found the

body. He said, 'I looked through the doorway and saw a woman lying face downwards at one end of the room. I ran and fetched Ronnie [his friend] ... and then we went to tell a bus man.' Edith was only twenty-seven, and she also had been living in a women's hostel in the same West Bar area. Her hostel landlord had not seen her since the Friday, and her body was found on Sunday.

The man must have been at least partially convincing, because he claimed the killer had gone to Rhyl and the police gave Smedley the benefit of the doubt, going with him to Rhyl to try to find the killer. Nothing came of that. Not long after, Smedley told the truth to his sister.

The killer had one more story to tell in order to try to create some kind of desperate extenuating circumstances around the vicious murder. He said that he had had sex with Edith but then she had told him that she had a venereal disease, so this information prompted him to attack her, and he lost control in his rage.

None of this achieved anything that would save him from the scaffold; he was hanged by the Wade-Kirk duo in August 1947. Smedley had been told that he had no chance of an appeal, but in sheer desperation he tried the last ploy – a letter to the Home Secretary asking for a pardon. As Sheffield writer, David Bentley, has written in his book *The Sheffield Hanged*, 'The execution attracted no interest, not a single person being present when the statutory notices were posted outside.'

Towards the end of his short period in office, Wade had two victims, both called Moore. The first, Alfred Moore, was guilty of killing two police officers and so his story made all the papers and provoked those elements of society in favour of retaining the death penalty to insist that for the murder of police officers, hanging should always be the sentence. In the 1957 Homicide Act, there were five definite instances in which hanging should be applied and one was 'Any murder of a police officer acting in the execution of his duty or of a person assisting a police officer so acting.' Moore's killing had done much to put that sentence there.

The double murder took place in the most unlikely of places: the quiet suburb of Huddersfeld, Kirkheaton, at Whinney Close Farm. Even today, this is an area in which older property with ample gardens stand side by side with newer suburban developments, quiet, occupied by families, and on the edge of the town, not far from the fields and smallholdings around Lepton.

In July 1951 Alfred Moore was a smallholder there, keeping poultry. But he also had a sideline in burglary to earn some extra cash. He was evidently not very skilled in his criminal activities and the police soon had him marked for observation. On 15 July the police surrounded his little homestead with the intention of catching him with stolen goods on him or on his property.

It was a stake-out that went badly wrong. In that very peaceful early morning of the Sunday, shots were fired in Kirkheaton and as officers moved around in the dark, trying to communicate and find the source of the gunfire, it was discovered that two officers had been shot: Duncan Fraser, a detective inspector, was found dead, and PC Jagger was severely wounded.

It was learned that Moore was holed up inside his house and it was inevitable that he would eventually be captured. The only glitch in the investigation was that, as a revolver had been used in the killings, a revolver had to be found on the person or the property and that never happened. Moore had a shotgun. But despite the use of a metal-detector, a revolver was never located.

But of course, PC Jagger was still alive so there was a witness to the dreadful events of that early morning. From his hospital bed, Jagger picked out Moore from a line-up. In a stunning piece of bravery and high drama, a specially formed court was formed at the hospital so that Jagger, almost certainly dying, could testify. Moore was tried for murder in Leeds; PC Jagger died just the day after giving evidence. Wade and Allen were busy at Armley once again.

Wade's last hanging was more mundane: simply a case of a man killing his wife's mother – the woman who had stood in the way, as he saw it, of his happiness with Maureen Farrell of Wombwell. Her mother, Clara, became an object of hatred for the young man, Alec Wilkinson, only twenty-two years old. On 1 May 1955, Wilkinson had a great deal to drink and worked himself up to a mood of extreme violence and enmity towards Clara Farrell.

Not long after their marriage, Alec and Maureen had been under pressure, and the relationship between Alec and his mother-in-law was one of extreme emotional tension, she apparently always criticising him and making it clear that he was worthless (at least that is how he claimed to see the situation). On the fateful day when he walked up to the front door of the Farrell's home in Wombwell, he had a burning spite in him and he was in a mood to use it. First he sprang on Clara and punched her and then slammed her head on the floor.

But such was the man's fury that he went for a knife in the kitchen, stabbed her, and then did something that suggests a psychosis as well as a drunken fit: he piled furniture on the woman and set fire to it. Wilkinson left as someone came to try to put out the fire, but later Alec confessed and one of his statements was that he was not sorry for what he had done. There was an attempt to demonstrate provocation, and even a petition to save him, but Wilkinson was found guilty of murder at Sheffield and sentenced to hang. This time, on Wade's last appearance as hangman, when he was becoming too ill to do any more, his assistant was Robert Stewart.

Steve Wade returned to Doncaster and lived on Thorne Road, Edenthorpe. He had been a café proprietor and he operated Wade's Motor Coaches. He retired in 1955 and died just over a year after hanging Wilkinson, on 22 December 1956, at Doncaster Royal Infirmary. The only teasing question about his official obituary is this note: 'Buried at Rosehill Cemetery (unconsecrated) in Doncaster. He seems to have been a very reticent character. Syd Dernley, who worked with him, said simply, 'Wade was a quiet man and said no more than hello when Kirky did the introductions.'

Perhaps the laconic Albert Pierrepoint said the simplest and best thing about Steve Wade, in his biography, *Executioner:*

Pierrepoint, when being questioned about his work. He was asked, 'Do you know whether any of those who are at present on the list [the official Home Office list of hangmen] have ever carried out an execution?'

Pierrepoint replied, 'Only one, and he has done five or six. Steve Wade, a good, reliable man.'

CHAPTER 28

Curiosities

That is when she is blowing into my bowels …

E very survey of regional crime across the land will have its share of odd cases: those bizarre sidelights to the main show of crime history. After all, not all criminal offences are desperate, horrible and bloody. There is tragedy in many tales, of course, but also some laughs and some scratching of the head. This is a selection of some of the strangest or most unusual.

Bewitched

Early in the nineteenth century, a surgeon from the Doncaster area wrote to a local paper to inform the world of a bizarre tale of alleged witchcraft. It seems that a Yorkshireman of seventy-eight went to both surgeon and police with this tale of woe. The man had given evidence at an inquest into the death of the husband of a certain Mary Anne Tinker. Though the wife was never charged with any offence, she put a hex on the old man, saying, 'You will never be the man you are, no more!'

He told the doctor that the lady began to be violent against him:

> *The first time she attacked me she took me in the back part of my neck and driv me across the house … I could not see her, but I knew it was her. Some weeks back she wrought me dreadful harm. I could not keep a limb still nor nothing. She often pinches my hands and she puts wind into me … That is when she is blowing into my bowels. She puts things into the room I sleep in … I can't see 'em but I hear 'em … She is a witch, a proper witch, but how she do it, only the dear Lord knows.*

The good doctor appears to have taken no action against the 'witch'.

Poaching – Twentieth-Century Style

By the 1920s, people were poaching using cars rather than always creeping about in the undergrowth at night and having fun with the gamekeeper. In 1933, three men in a car, using a false licence and false plates, went on a poaching spree but were detected and the good people of Doncaster set up a barricade of farm carts to stop them. But it was not all laughs: there was a charge of one of the men, William Birtles, a scrap-dealer shooting at police. Luckily for him he was found not guilty but he and his accomplices were still in trouble: Birtles was given twenty months in prison and his friends each had six-months sentences.

A poacher appeared at Doncaster Police Court in 1921 charged with assaulting a police sergeant. He was also allegedly drunk and disorderly and was poaching. The incident involved a chase across the countryside, with a magistrate, Mr Skiffner, joining a police sergeant in pursuit of a drunken poacher called Perkins who had assaulted the sergeant. Finally, the villain was caught and, only after the officer applied his truncheon to Perkins' head, was an arrest made.

The drunken poacher had to pay a £3 fine and four months in gaol for his drunken day out with a gun.

A 'Domestic' with Long Term Results

In 1954, there was a domestic fight on Christmas Eve – a time fraught with family squabbles for many. But this time it was not so amusing for an Adwick woman who was badly scarred. She was hit on the face with a teapot and her jaw was broken. Two family members were grappling in the kitchen in the ruck, one individual had a pan of boiling water as a potential weapon but it was knocked from his hand.

We have to feel for the lady in question who was scarred though: there was nothing slapstick about her wound – she needed ten stitches, two teeth were loosened and a filling knocked out.

The Conjurer

Back in 1778, a Doncaster workman had saved seventeen guineas and stashed them in his house, not trusting any bank to look after it. The money was then stolen. His method of detecting the thief was to employ a town crier to proclaim the name of the thief after he had consulted the famous Copper Street Conjurer, a man whom he believed would reveal the name of the culprit. Amazingly, the night after this intention was proclaimed, eleven guineas were secretly returned.

The conjurer's business had a rapid up-turn after that.

Dawson the Poisoner

Daniel Dawson was hanged in Cambridge for poisoning racehorses at Newmarket – and he also plied his trade at Doncaster. This is a horrible offence, of course, but unfortunately was not uncommon in Regency times. The tale began in 1809 when two horses died of poisoning after drinking from a horse trough. Then later the favourite for the Claret Stakes was 'nobbled'. The owner, Richard Prince, was warned, but saw nothing unusual. Playing safe, he watered horses from another trough but forgot one day, and four horses died. Dawson was the main suspect because he was in the pay of bookies. What emerged was that the rogue had been busy with that sort of practice at Doncaster as well. There were men up north after his blood, and no one wept as he walked out onto the scaffold.

The Judge is Attacked

Judges travelling on the circuit routes between towns in the Assize courts were obviously in need of guards and escorts. In the centuries before the modern era they sometimes went on the road with hundreds of men to protect them, because sometimes gangs would be active and would attempt to prevent a trial of one of their number.

But in the Civil War period, an officer who had been discharged from Oliver Cromwell's army, called Peter de Beauvior, lay in wait for a judge called Baron Thorpe, at Doncaster. The problem was that he spoke to several men about his intentions, and that could have ruined his plan. But he had a gang of friends and they all stayed at the same inn that Thorpe would be staying at. Peter was ready for a scrap:

he carried four pistols, a dagger and a carbine. But he was more mad than sane and he was arrested before he could do any harm. The most amazing aspect of the story is that he was discharged without any real trouble, as people stood sureties for his future good behaviour.

A Crime Behind Bars

In the eighteenth century the great prison reformer John Howard toured and inspected all the gaols in the land; he was disgusted by York and other Yorkshire prisons, but then at Doncaster he was shocked to find that all day long the male and female prisoners were left to be mixed together. He wrote about Doncaster Gaol:

> *One of the vagrants at this time in the prison was a Scotch woman, who, having lost her husband and being just recovered from a serious illness, was travelling homewards in company with her little child. She complained bitterly of her situation. 'What could I do?' she said. 'I dare not steal – I liked not to beg – destitute and afflicted –what could I do but apply to the magistrates for a pass? The consequence of this is that I am shut up for a week in prison and exposed perhaps to the worst and most vicious of men ...'*

Bigamists

In 1880, George Coop married two women within a space of two months. He stood in court before the judge, who said, 'In marrying this woman within two months of your previous marriage you not only violated the law, but inflicted a very grievous injury upon her, because I hold that in inducing a woman to marry him, by representing to her that he is a single man, and can make her a respectable home, is an offence which is very little short of the crime of rape.' He said it was his duty to give a severe penalty, and he gave him a prison sentence of twelve months. In fact, he really wanted to give Coop penal servitude, but explained: 'I have been told that the prisoner had been a hard-working man and deeply regretted what he had done.'

In contrast, Sarah Ann Roberts appeared in Doncaster Police Court in 1871 charged with 'intermarrying' – having wed William Clark in Yorkshire, a spirit merchant's traveller, while having a husband in Shrewsbury, a Mr Edwin Roberts. He was, it was confirmed, still alive. She was bailed and later was given a short term inside. Her charms as a vocalist clearly brought her many gentlemen friends, and there were problems when her love of marriage became too powerful and led to a session in front of the judge.

Nasty Robberies

Being placed along the main route north, Doncaster and the surrounding area has had its share of highway robbery. A typical case is that of Enoch Price and Henry Batty, who, in 1850, assaulted and robbed one Ann Lister. They stole a batch of assorted items, including a bag, some candles and some bottles. It was not much of a haul, considering that they went to so much trouble. Mrs Lister left Bentley to travel at night just the short distance into Doncaster.

Price fancied himself as a modern-day Dick Turpin, putting a handkerchief over his face and then taking out two pistols. He put one barrel to the head of Mrs Lister and said he would blow her brains out if she didn't give them what money she had. The other man stayed well back and they were both nervous. When they thought someone was coming they grabbed the lady's bag and ran off. Their day of criminal adventure left them with a bag of almost worthless objects.

There was a third man, called Hogg, and he was happy to be the 'grass' for the Crown. He explained how the robbery was planned – very badly of course. It was a ridiculous tale of three incompetents, but of course, they terrified the woman, and gaol was waiting for them.

Of course, there are many tales like this. In 1860 a 'boothpuller' or haulier, from Barnsley, called John Wells, delivered his freight to Doncaster, took his money and set off home on his cart. About half a mile from Doncaster he met two men called John Matthewman and Joseph Shaw. He was asked first if he would swap his old horse for a donkey. He refused, and the two robbers set about him, stealing his cash – seventeen shillings. But matters in court at Doncaster were very confused, mainly because the haulier was a man with a bad character. Had he made up the fact that he was robbed?

The bench was of the opinion that Wells was probably not robbed, but was clearly assaulted. The highway robbers had a year inside. As for Wells, he was reluctant to prosecute again, naturally.

Many years before this, in 1763, a man called John Allen was let loose to rob around Doncaster. Two boxes were sent north from London in a wagon, and they had a massive quantity of valuable silk. After being delivered to Doncaster, the boxes were to go to Pitsmore, near Barnsley, but Allen went after them and took them, saying they were his. The robbery led to some rare detective work, because in London, the brother of the novelist Henry Fielding, Sir John, wrote to a Mr Wood at Doncaster to have the villain caught. He was, and back in London he was found guilty. It was a 'grand larceny' which meant he had a death sentence.

In 1759, a rogue called Edward Jewen was in trouble for stealing a good deal of silver, and he had disappeared. Witnesses spoke at the Old Bailey, saying they had seen the stolen items in the man's room. But where was he? A woman called Currie deposed that after adverts in the *Public Advertiser*, the thief had responded, writing to Mrs Currie and asking her to get him freed from Doncaster gaol, where he had ended up after being on the run. He came back to face the music and was found guilty. He must have thought there was a good chance he would have a light sentence, but he was wrong. He was sentenced to hang at Tyburn. Rogues such as he rarely trusted ladies in London, but his gullibility was the end of him. He appears to have been even more incompetent, because he had the folly to leave his booty down in London, hinting to anyone curious that he was likely to return anyway – if he ever got out of Doncaster.

We have to remember that at that time, when we had twice-yearly assizes, a person accused could spend a long time rotting in gaol, waiting for the judge, if his offence was a serious one.

He Blackmailed Dad

Some children are never grateful. Some are a nuisance, and others are an absolute pain. Such a one was a young man who had a delight in terrifying his father – but all was not what it seems, as the following account will show.

William Davis was a journalist (as he said himself) working in Leicester in 1914. His father lived at Edlington, and in court in April of that year, the Rev WL Davis explained that his son had been 'a source of annoyance' for many years. It had all gone too far, though, because now young William, twenty-five, was demanding money with menaces. The prosecution made it clear that William had been receiving a pound a week for a long time but 'would never work'. The father's case was that his son had never made the allowance sufficient for his needs, but instead, had tried to extort more money by blackmail.

A few weeks before the court hearing, a postcard had been sent to the Reverend with this curt message: 'You are not worth writing to. I shall protest against your canting hypocrisy. Preach better sermons.' On other cards the son had said that father had made his mother's life hell. In one message the abuse was very offensive: 'You have twisted me out of my money and abused me. You are a dirty scoundrel and caused me great expense. I expect it from a pig. You ought to be in a pigsty.'

There were accusations in the cards and letters that, as the report at the time said, would 'deprive the clergyman of his ecclesiastical living'. William said he had written to the Archbishop with very serious allegations about his father. The cards were addressed to the father in terms such as 'Greedy Guts' and 'Revd. W. Davis, Money-Grabber'. But sometimes the abuse was not simply on paper. When his mother and father were out walking at one time in Edlington, William appeared and shouted abuse and threats at his father. Police were called and William was arrested. There was evidence from a police constable that William had said, in the cell, 'I want some money or I will kill him before morning.'

In the witness box, the accused denied the threats and the statement of intended murder. He said, 'There has always been a difference between myself and my father which I could never understand, but some months ago I was informed by a relative that it was secretly known in the family that this man is not my father... My real father is a clergyman in Nottingham.' The 'journalist' was bound for Leeds Assizes, but it never progressed that far. The father had probably had enough of the 'dirty washing' in public, true or not.

The blackmail in this case seems to have taken second place: the emotional narrative behind the threats attracted the real media interest.

Slander Again

Sir Samuel Instone was a powerful man in 1927: he owned ships as well as a colliery, and he didn't like being called a 'Welsh swindler and a "twister". That is what Herbert Smith, president of the Miners' Federation of Great Britain called him in a speech at Askern. It was during the coal strike at the time, but Smith denied ever saying the words, in spite of his anger. His defence was that 'the words were not capable of the meaning given' and they there was no malice.

Surely it was a hard task to claim that those words had no malice. Instone had acquired control of Askern Colliery in 1918 and, at the time, the company was developing a pit near Doncaster, and this was becoming productive in the war years. In April 1926, Instone had gone to that pit as there had been a fall of coal, but it was decided that the pit would be re-opened, but with no terms of employment that would be an improvement on the conditions of 1910 when it was first started.

Hundreds of men were employed, but even so the number was only a third of the number of miners who would have normally worked there. The mine workers' union were not happy about all this. Smith addressed a meeting at the Picture House in Askern and on that occasion he said, 'About this Sir Samuel Instone. We always know if we hear of any trouble where it comes from – Askern, which is worked on nothing but a twist. This was only one of his twists. Don't leave it to a Welshman... A Welshman will never do you any good. Rely on

Cook [AJ Cook, another miners' leader] and myself...If I want trouble I can always get it from a Welsh swindler.'

That is definitely explicitly with malice and prejudice, and the audience in Askern had some Welsh people in it, who obviously responded, making Smith say, 'I do not mean you fellows, but the owners of the pit...'

Although Smith was defended by the great barrister Sir Patrick Hastings, he lost. A thousand pounds in damages was awarded to Sir Samuel (worth about £30,000 today). Through modern eyes, it appears to have been a very risky and rash statement to make, knowing just how many Welsh miners there have always been, across virtually all mining communities. His attempt to qualify his words must have lowered him in the estimation of many of his members. It is surely the case that the speaker thought he would be popular with everyone if he criticised the powerful people, the Lords of Industry, in front of the workers. His judgement was badly wrong.

Strange Thefts

The magistrates' court in Doncaster over the years has seen some odd cases of petty theft, some serious and some bizarre. One crook stole a half sovereign but the investigation and police procedure had to be the same as a large-scale operation. A police officer had to travel to Ireland to catch the thief and to bring him home. When the man was finally standing in court to hear his punishment, the result was a fine of just £1.

Thefts recorded include a stone of India rubbers and 274 marbles. But some offences were mysterious, as the case of a little boy who stole two dozen copies of *The Catholic Times*. As Ernest Pettifer notes in his memoirs, old crime records demand a challenge to the vocabulary, as in the case of a theft of 'two backskins'- apparently these were strong jackets worn by pit-sinkers to protect them from falling stones as they sank shafts. There is a whole language devoted to mining of course, and those words have entered the criminal records.

Offenders in the courts through the ages have been guilty of the theft of almost anything. The heart of that particular urge to commit a crime is the old maxim: 'I did it because I could.' The opportunist criminal was always in the Doncaster court, as he was everywhere.

A Million to One Chance

Of all the cases in the area under scrutiny here, a story from the 1920s has to be a contender for the most unusual. It is a story of two drivers. The first man bought a car in Leicester and went to collect it, setting off from Bradford. When he arrived and saw the car, there were no number plates on the vehicle. He was told that there were no plates because he had never requested that the garage do the registering for him. The way out of the dilemma was to paint some plates on. The mechanic did just that, despite the fact that such a thing was very questionable. But it was all agreed and the buyer went away in his new car.

That same day, at night, another driver in Doncaster, going to Hull saw someone trying to do some repairs to his vehicle on the roadside and stopped to help. The lights on the car had failed. But when the good Samaritan looked at the car, he saw the plates and said, 'Hey, you've got my registration number!' The man who had been too eager to get his new car home and had allowed the number to be put on, had the most stunningly bizarre bad luck. As Ernest Pettifer wrote about the case:

> *The car with the forged plates had come to a stop on the one short stretch of road over which the two drivers each had to pass on their respective journeys ... the lights had failed just long enough to detain the man from Leicester ... then came on at just the right moment to show the forgery ...*

This was the kind of story that was destined to appear in a collection of paranormal tales, rather than criminal ones, but whatever the place where it is told, it is irresistible.

The Horrors of Animal Cruelty

In 1907, a Mr Reginald Martindale wrote to *The Times* to bring the attention of cruelty to horses to the reading public. He wrote, 'It is a grievous blot on the honour and humanity

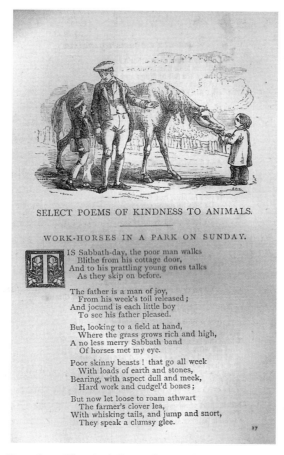

SELECT POEMS OF KINDNESS TO ANIMALS.

WORK-HORSES IN A PARK ON SUNDAY.

'IS Sabbath-day, the poor man walks
  Blithe from his cottage door,
And to his prattling young ones talks
  As they skip on before.

The father is a man of joy,
  From his week's toil released ;
And jocund is each little boy
  To see his father pleased.

But, looking to a field at hand,
  Where the grass grows rich and high,
A no less merry Sabbath band
  Of horses met my eye.

Poor skinny beasts ! that go all week
  With loads of earth and stones,
Bearing, with aspect dull and meek,
  Hard work and cudgel'd bones ;

But now let loose to roam athwart
  The farmer's clover lea,
With whisking tails, and jump and snort,
  They speak a clumsy glee.

Poem from Chamber's Journal, 1861. Author's collection

of this country that England with her proud boast of the love of horses should be the nation that bears the ugliest record in the decrepit horse traffic.' In the Edwardian years this was a hot topic in the media and so was clearly a widespread abuse, and, of course, a criminal offence. An organisation called the Dumb Friends' League was formed to try to combat this abuse.

Doncaster, being one of the most celebrated parts of England for horses, both in racing and down the pit, unfortunately had its share of cruelty cases. Pony drivers were often in the courts accused of cruelty to their ponies. In one local case, a pony was beaten so brutally that it died, and another story was of a pony having an eye knocked out.

Two Acts had been passed in the nineteenth century to try to deter the ill-treatment of animals: in 1835 the Cruelty to Animals Act tried to protect cattle and also bears and dogs (from the sports of baiting bears and dog-fight pits); then in 1849 the scope was widened to have an impact on the treatment of all animals. By 1910 there were questions in parliament specifically about horses.

The traffic in decrepit horses was by that time something of genuine social concern. The Earl of Mayo said in the House of Lords: 'Let me tell your Lordships what is going on at the moment… There is a large class of horse valued at under £5 by the Board of Agriculture, shipped to Holland… because Holland only exports horses for food.' He went on to describe the trade, with animals being taken to the ports of Hull, Goole, Newcastle, Leith and London. One of the worst instances was a man from the Doncaster area who had taken two ponies tied to the back of his cart, from his home to Goole, and sold the animals to a trader who then attended to the rest of the process. The horses were maltreated and half-starved. Sadly, that was not a rare occurrence.

Through modern eyes, the whole business is repulsive, but it has to be recalled that the definition of animals at the time was still firmly entrenched in the notion of their being 'chattels' – as disposable as a wooden box. At least the questions in the Lords in 1910 was a massive leap forward compared with the Regency a century before, when animals were the victims in hundreds of different varieties of gambling and cruelties in pubs and barns.

Red Roger and Robin Hood

It would be strange to have a collection of tales about criminals around Doncaster without including Robin Hood, particularly now that the airport bearing his name has given the area a definite attachment to that outlaw of legend.

Many writers seem to agree that Elizabeth de Staynton killed Robin Hood, who supposedly lies buried at Kirklees

Priory, near Hartshead. But did Elizabeth kill Robin? The beginning of this is in the old ballad, *The Death of Robin Hood*, from a first text found in 1786, though much older. This poem has the element of Robin firing an arrow at the Priory, to mark the spot where he will have to stop and have help, for he is badly wounded. The tradition here is that the prioress was his relative: 'But I have a cousin lives down below.'

He says that he will be safe there:

The dame prior is my aunt's daughter
and nie unto my kinne;
I know she would do me no harme this day,
For all the world to winne.

But in the poem, she bleeds him until he is virtually dead: 'She laid the blood-irons to Robin's vain ... and well then wist good Robin Hood/ treason was within.'

What had supposed to have happened is that she lets some blood, ostensibly to treat him for his feverous condition, but she over-bleeds him and he is very weak. Then she calls for the villain 'Red Roger', who finishes Robin off. One view of this is that there is religious symbolism at work, and AJ Pollard puts it this way:

The prioress has been transformed into a widow. To some extent it would make more sense if Robin's nemesis had been a widow who had taken a vow of chastity, but broken these with her accomplice. Be that as it may, the short version clearly identifies his betrayer as the prioress.

There appears to be some substance in the details of the tale, including the evil Roger. This is said to be Roger of Doncaster (spelt 'Donkesly' in the first version). Research has made it possible that he was from Sprotborough, and the references to him in the fourteenth century are interesting; and he has a link with Sherwood, as he owned land there.

Doncaster clearly wants to claim Robin as its own, and so there has to be a glance in the direction of a supposed villain: Red Roger, the man who has given the link to the place.

Sources and Bibliography

There has not been a great deal of material in print on crime in Doncaster history. As usual with such sources, the writing has been scattered and piecemeal, but in one way that is an advantage. It means that the writer has to reconstruct the stories from eclectic sources and make a sense of drama come through. Nevertheless, there have been some major cases, notably the 1829 betting room robbery, and the two principal executions in the twentieth century. For the former, historians have to rely on contemporary records across the press and in trial reports. Apart from the strain on the eyes, the challenge there is to sort out the likely truth of events from the anecdotes and the prejudice of reporters. But one of the pleasures of crime history is that, surprisingly for many, not all the stories in that area are grim and gruesome, and there have been surprises on the way.

The sources therefore range from small booklets from local writers to massive reference works, and I hope that this book will perhaps spark some interest from other crime historians in the Doncaster area, as there are still many more 'foul deeds' stories to be told. Without monographs and learned articles from specialists, it would be very difficult to assemble a solid casebook for the general reader.

Books

Bailey, Catherine, *Black Diamonds: the rise and fall of an English dynasty* (Penguin 2007)

Barber, Brian, *A History of Doncaster* (Phillimore 2007)

Baylies, Carolyn, *The History of the Yorkshire Miners 1881–1918* (Routledge 1993)

Benson, EF, *As We Were: a Victorian Peepshow* (Penguin 2001)

Chalmers, Patrick R, *Racing England* (Batsford 1939)

Cyriax, Oliver, *The Penguin Encyclopaedia of Crime* (Penguin 1996)

Dean, Joseph, *Hatred, Ridicule and Contempt: a book of libel cases* (Macmillan 1953)

Dernley, Syd, *The Hangman's Tale: memoirs of a public executioner* (Macmillan 1990)

Eddleston, John J, *The Encyclopaedia of Executions* (John Blake 2002)

Emsley, Clive, *Crime and Society in England 1750–1900* (Pearson Education 1996)

Fielding, Steve, *The Executioner's Bible* (John Blake 2007)

French, Yvonne and Squire, John, *News from the Past 1805–1887* (Gollancz 1930)

Fulford, Roger, *Votes for Women: the story of a struggle* (Faber and Faber 1958)

Hamilton, Dick, *Foul Bills and Dagger Money: 800 years of Lawyers and Lawbreakers*
(Cassell 1979)

Harris, Richard (Ed), *The Reminiscences of Sir Henry Hawkins* (Nelson 1910)

Hattersley, Roy, *The Edwardians* (Little, Brown 2004)

Haynes, Alan, *The Elizabethan Secret Services* (Sutton Publishing 1992)

Herbert, Barry, *Ticket to the Gallows and other villainous tales from the tracks*
(Silver Link 2001)

Hibbert, Christopher, *The Roots of Evil: a social history of crime and punishment*
(Sutton Publishing 2003)

HMSO, *Markets and Fairs in England and Wales*, 1928

Liddington, Jill, *Rebel Girls: their fight for the vote* (Virago 2007)

Marjoribanks, Edward, *The Life of Sir Edward Marshall Hall* (Gollancz 1929)

Moorhouse, Geoffrey, *The Pilgrimage of Grace* (Phoenix 2002)

Nield, Basil, *Farewell to the Assizes* (Garnstone Press 1972)

Norway, Arthur H, *Highways and Byways in Yorkshire* (Macmillan 1903)

Owens, Andy and Ellis, Chris, *Killer Catchers* (Blake 2004)

Pettifer, Ernest W, *The Court is Sitting* (Clegg and Sons 1940)

Rede, Thomas Leman, *York Castle* (J Saunders 1829)
Rutherford, Sarah, *The Victorian Asylum* (Shire 2009)
Shore, W Teignmouth, *The Baccarat Case* (Hodge, Notable British Trials 1932)
Whitbread, J R, *The Railway Policeman:the story of the constable on the track* (Harrap 1961
Yorkshire Archaeological Society: *Quarter Sessions Records of the West Riding,* 1945

Archival Material
Steve Wade MSS. In Doncaster Archives: DZ MZ 65/1, letter from Churchill and notes on several executions, including the Richter material.

Articles
Newton, Gerald, 'Germans in Sheffield 1817–1918', *German Life and Letters,* Vol. 46 January 1993 pp 83–101

Periodicals
Yesterday Today, Local History Newsletter, edited by Carol Hill, Doncaster Central Library, Issue 44, August 2004
Annual Register, 1829 and 1839
Fact
Illustrated Police News
Notes and Queries
Past and Present
Punch Library in Wig and Gown
Social History
True Crime

Newspapers
British Nineteenth Century Newspapers
Daily Graphic
Evening Chronicle
Guardian Gazette 1927
The Times Digital Archive

Websites
www.conisbroughcastle.org.uk/education

www.infoplease.com/dictionary
www.southwellminster.co.uk
ww.timesonline.co.uk
www.wikipedia.org
http://yourarchives.nationalarchives.go.uk

Illustrations
The images from Doncaster Council, kindly provided by Dr Charles Kelham, are referenced at AB/RACE/69 at Doncaster Archives.

The original artwork is by Vicki Schofield, as credited in the text.

Credit for the use of the map illustration in the railway story is to Cassini Publishing (see www.cassinimaps.com)

Index